A THEOLOGY OF PROTEST

BERNARD HÄRING

A Theology of

FARRAR, STRAUS AND GIROU

NEW YOR

PROTEST

Contents

Introduction

During the first week of the extraordinary two-week Synod of Bishops in October 1969, the press and television devoted almost as much attention to the group of priests (*prêtres solidaires*) meeting in Rome as they did to the bishops themselves. These priests were expressing solidarity with the successor of St. Peter and the College of Bishops, as well as nonviolent protest against the postponement of reforms which in their eyes are more urgently needed than ever. They felt and feel that their protest against outdated structures and obsolete concepts of authority is a necessary and integral part of their expression of solidarity with the church. Paradoxically, many protests and forms of protest today reveal a sincere concern for institutions that are not functioning properly. Though these priests were not able to agree among themselves on exactly what kind of reforms they were striving for, they clearly stated that in their opinion the ideas and proposals put forth by the progressive bishops at the Synod were too mild and overly cautious.

Both in Washington, D.C., and in Florence the confrontation between archbishop and priests seems to have become practically institutionalized. Is there any point in keeping things in a turmoil indefinitely? Who are the more effective protestors—those who protest on behalf of more freedom and reforms, or those who protest against changes or even the desire for change? I found myself during the recent Synod seated for half an hour at a Belgian TV broadcast between a soft-spoken worker-priest, one of the *prêtres solidaires,* and the French journalist Pierre Debray, who said that he was in Rome during the Synod in order to "protest against the protesting priests." In fact, his books and statements all breathe a kind of violent protest against nonviolent forms of protest, and represent a violent conservative reaction to any protest in favor of structural changes.

In Prague, for the time being at least, it seems that political protests have died down, yet surely this is a sign not of progress and tranquillity but of despair and resignation—unless, of course, we are on the verge of witnessing a new explosion of indignation. The student protests that are going on throughout the free world arise from the fact that students are vitally interested in the functions of their universities and refuse to give up hope that needed changes will be made. Confrontations and protests are still going on in the church. Some people deplore them, yet would the situation be healthy if such protests were to be effectively squelched by disciplinary action, or if they faded away through indifference without having achieved any of their goals?

What hopes or what fears should the present worldwide wave of protests inspire in us? Can the phenomenon be regarded as a useful or even necessary sign of progress? Will it eventually fade away, or will it subvert the present social order only to end, as the Marxist revolution has ended in many countries, as a kind of mummified, violence-permeated establishment, an establishment of the violent status quo dedicated to suppressing most human rights?

The reply to these questions will, to a great extent, depend on the way we view and interpret the real meaning of the protest movement and respond to it or allow ourselves to become involved. No doubt there are quite a number of negative aspects about the present wave of protests. Yet how can they be entirely positive when they are, to a large extent, caused by very unhealthy situations and at best by only a partial awareness of the real causes and interrelationships of those situations? There is danger in violence and in the psychosis of protest. Even the best-motivated energies and forms of protest can become misdirected and can be abused by unscrupulous leaders and manipulators. This will most likely occur if we are not alert to the nature of the precious energies being released, cannot appreciate the desire for authenticity, or ignore the widespread consensus that pious words without appropriate structural changes are an affront to human nature. Unquestionably, there is in the church today a genuine widespread interest in social reform, a heartfelt need for co-responsibility at all levels, as so eloquently expressed by Cardinal Suenens, and a great yearning for progress and maturity. People are quite ready today, as never before, to make real sacrifices on behalf of a just cause; they feel impelled to raise their voices against all forms of ecclesiastical and worldly pharisaism.

A totally new dimension and effectiveness has been given the protest movement by modern means of mass communication. Information about any form of protest that may be of interest to the public is immediately televised and reported on to a worldwide audience, and helps to increase the intensity and repercussions of the phenomenon. Any paternalistic or violent reaction on the part of those being challenged, or authoritarian protests against protest, only tend to promote more fervor and determination. Only a realistic response displaying a desire for dialogue and a willingness to undertake deep-seated reforms can effectively counter the waves of protest, challenge and confrontation today.

There should be a frank acknowledgment that the economic, cultural, social and political changes now taking place are dynamic and cannot be stopped. The fact that youth and the more progressive elements in society are becoming increasingly impatient with the violent methods used by reactionary authorities, with the notorious failure of professional "brakemen" to apply the brakes effectively, and with the exasperating immobilism of scandalously outdated structures tells us that we are going to have to live with the phenomenon of protest, whether we like it or not, for quite a while.

If we do not learn how to make the best possible use of the opportunities afforded by this phenomenon, we will not fare very well. I consider it one of the most imperative tasks at the present time for the social sciences and theology to study the real meaning of this striking aspect of life today. Those who believe that they can deal with it in a paternalistic fashion, by simply repeating the tired "solutions" of a former century, are playing with fire. Admittedly, a realistic confrontation with this new reality will not be possible without incurring certain risks and making mistakes. But there is less risk in taking action than in simply waiting for the flood to overwhelm our inertia.

The various chapters of the present book were not composed in an ivory tower. Most of them took shape as a result of discussions with youth, university protestors, laymen, priests and theologians protesting against church structures and the way church authority is exercised, with men and women of all ranks, in other words, avant-garde and rearguard bishops and cardinals. These contacts inevitably led to serious reflection on my part. What are the basic problems involved, the criteria by which to judge them, and the ways by which we can make the best possible use of the present situation? What does Divine Providence intend to teach us in all this?

The starting point must be the apparent contradiction we find in the Gospel between revolutionary dynamism on the one hand and its call for nonviolence on the other. The Gospel makes clear what the most effective kind of protest against all forms of inertia and maintenance of the status quo should be, and declares that this is the only way to free humanity from the slavery of war and exploitation (chapters I and II).

It is an illusion and perversion of the truth to think that

any bare act of violence can effectively lead to real liberation. Freedom is an undivided good; and as such it is possible only in a community and by joint effort at all levels of society (chapter III).

Any discussion about protests and efforts to weigh goals and methods of protest inevitably leads to fundamental questions about man's striving for maturity and the function and role of conscience (chapters IV and V).

The Christian moralist naturally has to look for proper moral criteria. He also has to free himself from all kinds of short-cut or cut-and-dried judgments about moral problems. We must endeavor to reach the deeper social causes, the meaning of the social processes and the interdependence of all these factors. It will then be easier to talk realistically about moral problems and to seek remedies for those evils which caused the outbursts of protest. Thus we have to try to isolate and stress the positive side of the energies being displayed and evaluate in this light the present opportunities in the world and within the church (chapters VI and VII).

Those theologians who have the courage to confront *objectively* the many-faceted problem of protest, as we see it today, will be forced to admit that both they as theologians and the science of theology as such are being challenged as never before. Both can only benefit from a sincere acceptance of the challenge (chapter VIII).

The strength, character and content of our hope will determine the sincerity and forcefulness with which we, as Christians, exercise our prophetic role by challenging the immobilism and the inertia of structures as well as the wrong turnings which protest movements may be taking (chapter IX).

Parts of this book were first published in a paperback edition in Italian, *La Contestazione dei Non Violenti* (Morcelliana, 1969). Parts were published in German, but most of the book was originally written in English. I want to express my hearty thanks to Professor Arthur B. Crabtree of the Theology Department of Villanova University for translating those parts that first appeared in German; and to Mr. John Chapin for the translation of chapter II from the Italian. I am particularly indebted to Sister Gabrielle L. Jean, Professor of Psychology at Rhode Island College, and greatly appreciate her help in the final editing of the whole work.

Bernard Häring

Rome
November 1969

A THEOLOGY OF PROTEST

I

Nonviolence: The Gospel Means Revolution

The person in power is always inclined to defend the status quo. Even servants of the church are at times rewarded with fat morsels by the rich and powerful, provided that their religious teachings and care of the faithful serve the cause of such vested interests. For example, if the church, in defending the right of private property, upholds current practices regarding the distribution of wealth and profits, the mighty rich are all too happy to support the church's charitable works, in much the same way one acknowledges the modest contribution of a doorman or concierge with a tip. For too long the Christian churches, concerned with defending their own status quo as a kind of sacred power-realm, have entered into much too intimate an alliance between "throne and altar."

The defense of the status quo can of course assume varying significance according to time and circumstance. It makes a difference whether one defends the status quo of a more or less democratic and healthy society against a minority seeking to dominate or overthrow it, or seeks to justify and safeguard the position of a small but wealthy dominant group. Similarly the case is different depending on whether one seeks to maintain the status quo in a static age which enjoys a relatively stable social order, or in a highly progressive age marked by profound changes. Martin Luther's ethic of vocation, according to which everyone should be content with the social status and lot in life to which he is born, was understandable in a former age when possibilities for advancement were extremely restricted—even nonexistent. Yet the converse of this ethic was espoused by Luther during the Peasants' Revolt when he sided with the princes and landowners.

Whenever the church aligned herself in times of revolution with the disintegrating system and attempted to suppress the emerging society by threats of anathema, she rendered a great disservice to herself. Not only did she gravely injure herself as an institution but she weakened the credibility of her message.

Rightly understood, Christianity is a force promoting peace and a revolution. It would be a mistake to regard Christianity merely as a social movement, or an uprising of slaves, or any other form of social unrest. Jesus emphatically corrected the mistaken notion of those admirers who re-garded him primarily as a national and social liberator: "My kingdom is *not* of this world" (John 18:38).

Christianity Means Revolution

Christ demands of his disciples a new way of thinking, a renewal of the mind, a reorientation toward new purposes and ideals. The newness is so great that it cannot emerge from man alone; it must emanate from God's grace. By this grace and the preaching of conversion, a man sure of him-self becomes profoundly shaken. The goal of total renewal, however, is never complete in this life. Christian life implies constant conversion, an unflagging concern for growth and intensification that means, ultimately, a new relationship to God, to one's neighbor and to one's whole environment. It is only through an entirely new relationship to our neighbor that we honor God, our common Father in heaven, and our Lord and Brother, Jesus Christ. In faith Christ is accepted not only as the Saviour of the soul and the hope of resurrec-tion; he is the Redeemer of the whole man in all of his relationships, and Redeemer of the world. Therefore, the redeemed man cannot remain indifferent to inequities in the world or unconcerned about the inhuman conditions of his fellow man.

Christianity as the religion of love cannot preach eternal salvation without regard for the well-being of all men, since the hope of salvation transcends the horizons of this earthly life and encompasses the whole of man. Its purpose is to heal him and his environment, i.e., the world in relation to man, but this depends on the full cooperation of the redeemed with the grace of God.

To be a Christian means to be on the move. Nothing is more repugnant to the biblical concept of Christianity than complacency or idle satisfaction with the status quo. The Christian today cannot be content with merely minor adjustments, for everything is measured by the highest ideal, by the ideal of God's love as manifested in Jesus Christ. The Christian can never remain satisfied with himself if he is to be a genuine disciple of Christ. By the same token, because of his love of neighbor, he cannot be satisfied with the condition of his environment, both in the church and in the world at large. We are on the way toward a heavenly Jerusalem but this pilgrimage does not mean a flight from present responsibilities. Our hope of perfect brotherhood must express itself not only in striving for greater love but in our seeking to bring about needed reforms in social conditions.

According to Christian social doctrine, there can be no genuine renewal of heart and mind without concern for social reform. Conversely, there can be no healthy and effective attempt to reform conditions without constant conversion of mind and attitudes. In this sense the true Christian is really the all-out revolutionary, the one who knows no rest or repose.

The Christian, however, never seeks to overthrow merely for the sake of overthrowing. He seeks greater love and a dynamic order of justice or righteousness. The means to the goal are often the way of the cross, but the purpose always remains love. Consequently, every step must be inspired by true love and measured against the one criterion: Can it be regarded as an expression of true love? Is it capable of promoting love on earth?

Power within the Christian Revolution

Most revolutionaries are concerned with gaining power over others, as individuals or groups. Many are obsessed by power; others sincerely trust that they can exercise power with justice. In proclaiming his revolution of love, Christ completely excluded for himself and for his apostles any thought of earthly power. Did the Exemplar intend completely to preclude the concept of power for Christians who are primarily concerned with the social and political spheres?

Power for the sake of power is of course a great evil. As soon as lust for power and the desire to dominate others come into play, both the maintenance of the status quo and the striving for reform and change become inwardly corrupt. Power should never become an end in itself. That is why social and political endeavors must be wrested from the hands of those who seek only power or principally power.

However, power is not evil in itself; it is good when it is sought and exercised so as to serve the common good. The purest form of power is that of truth and love. Whoever desires the triumph of truth and authentic love dare not remain "powerless." Passions that are not animated by love destroy, yet without the power of passion human love is ineffectual and unreal. Similarly, power without the ordering energy of love and righteousness is highly dangerous, whether it be in the hands of officials who cling to the old ways or in the hands of revolutionaries. Nevertheless, it is impossible to think of reform or even government without real power.

When we speak of power, we should not think only of police clubs or machine guns, and certainly not of concentration camps or atom bombs. There is power in the spoken and written word, a power of ideas, a power of peaceful alliances, a power of community which comes from common and freely acquired convictions. However, we cannot avoid the question: What kind of power do we need to oppose the raw violence of criminal rulers or disturbers of the peace? Merely the power of the word or of ideas? Dare we and should we use force in order to compel unjust power-wielders to accept just demands? How much force can we use without ourselves becoming obsessed with power and injustice? A portion of Christendom answers with the "paradox of powerlessness." The thesis of this answer is that the strongest power is the love which mobilizes, epitomizes and musters all energies, that love which triumphs even in defeat.

The Nature of Nonviolence

One must not be misled by the apparently negative formulation of "nonviolence," seemingly implying a solution by the complete renunciation of force. Nonviolence as an attitudinal method relies on the gentle but limitless power of love. Nothing can extinguish love. Nothing can be compared to the love which seizes the whole man, pervades his thoughts and desires and guides all his actions. Nonviolence refers to the power of that courageous love that gathers, concentrates and combines all energies, the love that strives with might and main to overcome evil. Nonviolence resists all temptations and attempts on the part of violence to harvest successes and achieve triumphs which in reality spell the defeat of love.

The Christian disciple refrains from all violent action. He renounces revenge and even the victory of retributive justice insofar as he might himself become the victim of hatred or resentment. He protects himself against the assaults of hatred through the active manifestation of love. Paul describes this attitude in his exhortation: "If possible, so far as it lies with you, live at peace with all men. My dear friends, do not seek revenge, but leave a place for divine retribution; for there is a text which reads, 'Justice is mine, says the Lord. I will repay.' But there is another text: 'If your enemy is hungry, feed him; if he is thirsty, give him a drink; by doing this you will heap live coals on his head.' Do not let evil conquer you, but use good to defeat evil" (Rom. 12:18–21).

God alone is invulnerable in his love. His wrath and his punishment are always the purest expression of the righteousness of one who is love, whereas man is always in danger of allowing himself to be infected with hatred or resentment. He most effectively resists the evil that assails him from without or tempts him from within when he gathers together all the energies and attestations of love, like the housewife of old who gathered the glowing embers on the hearth so that there might always be a fire in the house.

It is of the nature of nonviolence in an evil world that the one who loves nonviolently and seeks righteousness endures blows and is ready to suffer. The power of love, of nonresistance, of courage and of patience, reveals itself eminently in face of the infectious powers of hatred, injustice and violent action. One who loves nonviolently and courageously resists injustice believes in the good which is in his assailant. Only a love which hopes all things is able to carry everything and endure anything without becoming bitter and seeking retaliation (I Cor. 13:4–7).

Is Nonviolence a Counsel Only?

For classical Marxism nonviolence is ultimately absurd. Karl Marx, in keeping with his dialectical materialism, believed that mankind could approach the final phase, the revolution of the proletariat and a classless society, only by way of an intensification of class hatred and class warfare. He hoped for the ultimate synthesis of harmonious righteousness and perfect peace through an explosion of hatred on the part of the long-oppressed classes subject to severe injustice. Nevertheless, even Karl Marx in his prophetic vision expected an earthly realm of harmony and nonviolence. There are many Christians who justify acts of violence by pointing to the otherworldliness of their hopes for peace. They argue that since total peace and total nonviolence will be granted to men only in "the other world," it would be presumptuous to take nonviolence as a rule and norm here on earth. But we must counter this by the objection that although we shall possess perfect love only after the consummation of all things, love is already here on earth the basic law for the disciples of Christ, whether or not other people live by it. The decisive question is to what extent the attitudinal methods of nonviolence can be deduced and established from the basic law of love, and to what extent they are obligatory.

Faith in the meaningfulness of nonviolence is an expression of the messianic peace already attained by those who are really reconciled with God. From our redemption and reconciliation by grace flows the power to exert ourselves for the messianic ordering of peace here on earth through the energies of that gentle, merciful love which embraces even our adversaries. Francis of Assisi, visiting the Sultan of Egypt in poverty and without weapons, is far more readily recognizable as a messenger of messianic peace than were the Crusaders.

The seven-times repeated "But I say to you" of the Sermon on the Mount is an expression of the messianic ordering of peace. It expresses the messianic consummation of the "law" and in this sense it possesses a normative value.[1] The interpretation of the normative character of the typical New Testament instruction results from an eschatological under-

---

[1] *Cf.* my essay, "The Normative Value of the Sermon on the Mount," in the *Catholic Biblical Quarterly,* XXIX (1967), 375-385, and my book, *Zusage an die Welt* (Bergen-Enkheim, 1968), 59-70.

standing of the Kingdom of Christ, which in this interim period is characterized by the tension between the "already" and the "not yet" of its fulfillment. The Christian who believes that the Kingdom of God is near proceeds in the direction of the sevenfold "But I say to you." The path is obligatory and clearly marked. Anyone who is guided merely or principally by the limiting commands, i.e., the restricting prohibitions, is running away from the Lord. Such persons are like the rich young ruler who indeed pleaded for eternal life, but was not willing to go the full way with the Lord.

However, since we are here concerned with a directive leading us to a goal, and not merely with a restriction, it is of utmost importance that in all earnestness we make a start and keep striving toward the goal. A directive provides no casuistic solution, like a limiting command. Nonviolence obliges us, somewhat in the manner of a command, to use simple and honest language, which is intended to render the oath superfluous but does not exclude it in all circumstances and absolutely. Just as it is senseless on the basis of the Sermon on the Mount to consider the casuistic questions of the legalities of marriage without doing everything possible for marriage preparation, marriage counseling and everything that can promote the stability of a marriage, so the directive to nonviolence forbids us to concern ourselves with the casuistry regarding just wars, the death penalty, police precautions and violent revolution without making nonviolence our fundamental concern and attempting first of all to mobilize all nonviolent methods for the conquest of injustice. Many canonists devote far more time and thinking to ways of annulling and dissolving mixed marriages than to ways of preserving the indissolubility and permanence of mixed marriages in the light of the Sermon on the Mount. This perverse perspective is found even more frequently as regards the directive concerning nonviolence. One considers how much violence is permissible and when it is called for, but blithely ignores the attitudinal methods of nonviolence. This violates the norms of the Sermon on the Mount.

Is Disciplined Force Permissible?

Anyone who wishes to build his house on the rock, i.e., on Christ's directive in the Sermon on the Mount, must certainly exclude the spirit of violence and all opportunistic methods of violent action such as war and armaments, physical or psychical torture, the beating of peaceful demonstrators and the death penalty. Nevertheless, I maintain that within the framework of the Sermon on the Mount, we can quite properly ask the question (on the presupposition that one has done everything possible to deal with evil nonviolently): When and to what extent should we resort to disciplined violence? Perhaps we should speak about the use of *force* rather than of "disciplined violence."

It would be a great blessing for all mankind if Christians would take Christ's injunctions seriously. One who in an extreme emergency is ready to renounce violence is far nearer to the Christian directive of the Sermon on the Mount than the one who exercises violence without first making every effort to apply the power of nonviolence.

Anyone who merely folds his hands and keeps out of the fray where fundamental questions of social justice and the welfare of men are at stake should not talk about nonviolence, at least not in the sense of Christ's teachings.

The Eastern Church and the Roman Catholic Church differ with respect to the interpretation of what the Sermon on the Mount has to say about the prohibition of divorce. The Eastern churches and many Protestant churches share the conviction that they are not contravening the directive of the Sermon on the Mount when they allow or tolerate the remarriage of a rejected marriage partner for whom there is no hope of a renewal of his or her first marriage. The Roman Catholic Church adheres literally and strictly to the principle of the Sermon on the Mount and makes its desire for clemency and mercy visible in other ways. Both branches of Christendom must face the question of conscience whether they have really done everything possible to strengthen the fidelity and durability of the marriage and, at the same time, to follow the Lord in mercy. We dare to hope that in similar fashion at least a significant portion of Christendom will follow the directive to nonviolence as faithfully as the Roman Catholic Church takes the law of the indissolubility of marriage, and that the rest of Christendom will limit the exceptions when violence is permitted as the lesser evil, just as rigorously as it limits the cases in which the remarriage of divorced persons is allowed. The question of nonviolence is for Christianity and the whole of humanity certainly of no less importance than the question of the indissolubility of marriage.

It is my conviction that the attempt to kill Hitler during the last war was justified; that is, it did not conflict with the Sermon on the Mount. I admit that the situation which led responsible men to resolve on such a step was induced by a massive violation of the Sermon on the Mount by the majority of people in general and by Christians in particular.

Whenever the question of the use of violence becomes acute, one must first ask whether all nonviolent methods have been exhausted to reduce the evil and resist the evil-doers. If anyone believes that the preservation of peace and tranquillity obliges him to use violence, he must first be sure of two things: (1) he must guard against becoming infected with the spirit of violent action and accordingly be ready to suffer injustice rather than become a victim of hatred, dragging others deeper into the morass of hatred; (2) he must examine himself carefully and conscientiously as to whether he is restricting himself to the unconditionally necessary minimum of violence in resisting violence and injustice.

It is at once the great evil and the great guilt of Christendom that we use violence with a good conscience and approach the abyss of a war of annihilation without the slightest attempt to think seriously about the inexhaustible energies of nonviolence.

The Success of Nonviolence?

Gandhi and Martin Luther King achieved considerable success with their promotion of the methods of nonviolence even though ultimately both lost their lives as the victims of violence. The abhorrence with which the whole world condemned the murderers of these apostles and witnesses of nonviolence is palpable evidence of the gradual victory of nonviolence everywhere when it is applied in a convincing, discriminating and passionate way. Wherever nonviolence has been unsuccessful, this has been mainly because there were too few apostles and witnesses. Even Christian moralists have failed to pay sufficient attention to this core teaching of the Sermon on the Mount. There is no use complaining about the inefficacy of medicine when we have not taken it or not taken it as prescribed.

The prototype of all nonviolence is Christ, who courageously withstood those who had the power to kill him. His sermons against the scribes, the Pharisees and the high priests were a powerful nonviolent protest against injustice and heartlessness. He knew that he would bring on conflicts and persecution. As Christians we believe that on the cross he won the decisive victory of love. Anyone who in his passionate struggle for righteousness and peace on earth commits himself to the path of nonviolence runs the risk of having to suffer and, according to earthly standards, of having to fail. Anyone, by contrast, who seeks tranquillity within his comfortably heated room has already missed the point; he equates nonviolence with lack of involvement. Anyone who, for a just cause, uses methods of violence runs the risk not only of perishing "by the sword" but also of becoming himself a victim of hatred and injustice, thus increasing the amount of hatred in the world.

The sole risk worth taking is the risk of nonviolence. It must be admitted, of course, that the ways of true apostles of nonviolence may in rare borderline cases diverge. There are some who believe that in the interests of justice and love a minimum of violence is permitted, while others give appropriate witness through their radical renunciation of violence and a lifelong effort to promote nonviolence.

The Second Vatican Council praises the last and ultimate victory of Christ, of the Prince of Peace who "slew hatred in his own flesh and poured the spirit of love into the hearts of men." It calls on all men actively to participate in moves toward peace. Injustice, violence and war threaten mankind, since men are sinners. "In the measure however in which men unite in love, they overcome violence." The praise of nonviolence is, however, cautiously expressed by the council, in keeping with the "not yet" of the ultimate fulfillment of the messianic peace: "Motivated by this same spirit, we cannot fail to praise those who renounce the use of violence in the vindication of their rights and who resort to methods of defense which are otherwise available to weaker parties, provided that this can be done without injury to the rights and duties of others or of the community itself."[2] Equally cautious is what the council has to say about objectors: "Moreover, it seems right that laws make humane provisions for the case of those who for reasons of conscience refuse to bear arms, provided however, that they accept some form of service to the human community."[3] The last phrase in no

[2] *Constitution on the Church in the Modern World*, Art. 78.
[3] *Ibid.*, Art. 79.

way weakens the affirmation, since our understanding of nonviolence can possess ethical value only when it is the attitude of those who place themselves at the service of the community and peace.

Violence and Social Injustice

Several groups of Christians concerned with social reform (e.g., *Témoignage chrétien, Christianisme social, Economie et Humanisme, Frères du Monde,* IDOC) have signed an appeal in which we read: "The revolutionary struggle finds its place within the perspective of the building of the Kingdom of God, without being identified with it. We recognize the right of every Christian and every man to participate in this revolutionary process, involving even armed conflict. We express as a community our support for those of the faithful who in consequence of their efforts have been rejected by their local church and who feel lonely in their faith."

This declaration has its justification in the monstrous misery produced by unjust exploitation and in the crying injustice committed by those who in the church align themselves with the exploiters, unilaterally condemning the exploited who seek change by violent means because peaceful means are likely to fail. Nevertheless, I have strong reservations with respect to the declaration itself. We should try to avoid completely using the expression "building the Kingdom of God" where the actions of men are concerned and particularly where the use of violence is being suggested. The very best that a man can do with respect to the Kingdom of God is to receive it in faith and to submit himself to its gentle and persuasive power. I believe that passionate acceptance of the Kingdom of God obliges us to oppose exploitation and denounce the unjust distribution of wealth everywhere in the world. As I see it, church communities have no right to apply a double standard; they ought not to condemn more strongly those who resort to violence in their struggle against an unjust status quo than those who resort to methods of force and violence in the defense of unjust conditions. Yet to me it seems dangerous to speak in such general terms about the use of violence, especially in the name of the Kingdom of God. This objection will have weight, however, only if we Christians succeed in awakening and marshaling the forces of nonviolence in order to put an end to the injustice which provokes violence.

One of the most complicated problems is the question to what extent Christians should join with men of other faiths and different attitudes in the struggle against injustice. There would be no particular problem if everybody desired nothing but the rooting out of injustice and the establishment of righteousness by morally acceptable means. But when some strive for a new dictatorship of one form or other in order to exploit people, or anarchy in order to terrorize everybody, or when some seek a right solution but nevertheless dedicate themselves opportunistically and immoderately to violent action, Christian participation may be gravely compromised. When it is a question of sound goals and means, Christians can of course join together with all men of goodwill. But a coalition with unjust powers must be totally excluded, whether the power be used in the service of an unjust status quo or in the service of an unjust revolution. However, if violence is employed either in a struggle to maintain an unjust order or against an injustice that cries to heaven, the apostle of nonviolence can only credibly keep his distance if, in a convincing manner, he is employing the greater healing energies of nonviolence for justice's sake.

The Second Vatican Council reminds us of the word of the apostle: "See, now is the time of grace; now is the time of salvation" (I Cor. 2:6). It sees a danger that unless humanity strives for peace more than it has so far, it may be approaching "the dark hour in which it experiences no other peace than that of the gruesome stillness of death." Precisely because of the immensity of this danger, the council warns: "Divine Providence urgently demands of us that we free ourselves from the age-old slavery of war."[4] That is possible only if we set in motion the positive energies of nonviolence in every area and with the entire resources of heart, will and mind. This means nothing less than a most radical kind of conversion, a most radical revolution, the kind that begins within each one of us and is calculated to join us all together in a relentless striving toward a more brotherly world.

[4] *Constitution on the Church in the Modern World,* Art. 80–81.

II

Protesting the Status Quo

The classical text on nonviolence is the Sermon on the Mount: "You have learned that they were told, 'An eye for an eye, and a tooth for a tooth.' But what I tell you is this: Do not set yourself against the man who wrongs you. If someone slaps you on the right cheek, turn and offer him your left. If a man wants to sue you for your shirt, let him have your coat as well. If a man in authority makes you go one mile, go with him two. Give when you are asked to give; and do not turn your back on a man who wants to borrow.

"You have learned that they were told, 'Love your neighbor, hate your enemy.' But what I tell you is this: Love your enemies and pray for your persecutors; only so can you be children of your heavenly Father, who makes his sun rise on good and bad alike, and sends the rain on the honest and the dishonest. If you love only those who love you, what reward can you expect? Surely the tax-gatherers do as much as that. And if you greet only your brothers, what is there extraordinary about that? Even the heathen do as much. You must therefore be all goodness, just as your heavenly Father is all good" (Matt. 5:38–48).

Prophetic Protest against the Status Quo

In presiding over history, God reveals his perfection, his holiness in mercy. As the prophet Hosea says: "How can I abandon thee, O Ephraim? I shall not act according to the fierceness of my wrath, because I am God and not a man: the holy one in the midst of thee, and I will not become angry" (Hos. 11:8–9). It is in this context that we must understand the term perfection and the idea of nonviolence.

The Sermon on the Mount is the strongest, most devastating but at the same time most constructive protest against the status quo. Central to its message is the seven-times repeated: "You have learned that they were told . . . but I say to you." Here Christ opposes his authority, his word, a dynamic word, a revolutionary word to a static order, a status quo characterized by minimalism, legalism, standpatism; in short, limitations, prohibitions and methods typical of this point of view: means of control and discrimination. "But I say to you . . ." If one believes in Christ, in the religious or moral sphere, it is no longer possible to advocate a violent defense of the status quo or a passive acceptance of it in a do-nothing sense. Jesus was merciful, "nonviolent," but he displayed a definite aversion toward the Pharisees, toward self-sufficiency, toward any system of thought or habit stamped by the status quo. It is true that Jesus says in the Sermon on the Mount: "I did not come to destroy the law," but he immediately clarifies what he means: "but to fulfill it," implying on-going movement. He was not content with what already was but was willing to accept a completely new situation. "The favorable time has come, the opportune time." The preaching of Jesus is that new time being fulfilled.

Chapter 19 of Matthew has similar or almost identical elements as those found in chapter 5; it therefore clarifies to some extent what Jesus means by perfection. For example, the word *teleios* with which he concludes the great sermon on nonviolence recurs in chapter 19 in the well-known story of the rich young man, typical representative of the well-intentioned men of the Establishment.

What must a person do if he wishes to gain eternal life? The young man lists with a certain degree of self-satisfaction all that he has done since his youth. He is very satisfied with himself but there is a certain goodness in him and Jesus loves him. Jesus then says: "If you wish to be perfect . . ." The word *teleios* (perfect) about which so many books have been written seems to mean here: if you wish to be a man of the fullness of times, if you wish to move from the old to the new age, if you wish to go the whole way from the status quo to the new demands. The new demands are radical. Man must no longer be a slave of the status quo, of wealth; he must not be attached to anything if he is to be fully free for Christ; and this also means free for his neighbor. "You are lacking something," as the synoptic evangelists Matthew, Mark and Luke put it.

There is another early text called the "Gospel of the Nazarene," a work dating from the beginning of the second century. It is not a canonical Gospel, but it dates from a time when there was still a living tradition about Jesus. It has the same story about the rich young man and says, as do the Gospel texts, that he had done everything that he should have done from his youth. And Jesus replied, a little less gently than in the synoptic texts: "You are a big liar. Your house is full of riches. Your brothers and sisters, the sons and daughters of Abraham, are dying of hunger, and you tell me that you have done all that love demands from your youth!" This text sheds light on the young man's idea of perfection. It shows him going away with sadness because *he does not wish* to leave behind him "what he had" in order to gain something "new": intimate friendship with Christ and hence the total gift of himself to others.

A closer look at the context is helpful here. Jesus explains what he had learned: the commandments that seem to be mere prohibitions, to which Jesus adds: "Love your neighbor as yourself," which is also the key to the commandments of the Old Testament. But Jesus, by his coming, makes clear that one can no longer be attached to his own things, to the status quo, to the situation as it has been until now, if he wishes to enter a new age.

The Prophetic Mission of Christ

In his Sermon on the Mount, in his whole life and death, Christ belongs to the prophetic tradition. This kind of protest is not violent, but it is all the more striking because of his humility, his service, his closeness to the humble people, his goodness. It is the most effective form of protest against the pride and self-sufficiency of the Pharisees or any other system of self-sufficiency. Jesus' whole life is a protest against self-complacency; he preaches *metanoia,* repentance: a complete transformation, not in the devotional sense confined to religious sentiment, but as *metanoia,* conversion, meaning at the same time a new relationship with God and with neighbor. *Metanoia,* change, is not possible without completely new relations with our neighbor and with all creatures. *Metanoia* is an infinitely dynamic concept.

Evidently, Christ did not reveal himself as a political, military or social leader. By his whole life Jesus declares that "my Kingdom is not of this world," but at the same time, Christ brings us the true revolution. A famous socialist said fifty years ago, "We socialists would have nothing to do if you Christians had continued the revolution begun by Jesus." Jesus also revolutionizes the relations between rich and poor. In the book of Proverbs, the Old Testament sages frequently advise against lending anything because it is so often lost. By contrast, in the text which deals with non-violence, Jesus says: "Give to anyone who asks and do not turn your back on anyone who wants a loan" (Matt. 5:42). The risk is obvious. Jesus knows that the Old Testament wise men, perhaps Arab sages whose many proverbs had been collected, warned consistently against risk; if he chose the same example, he does so deliberately in an opposite sense to encourage risk-taking. He who loves risks something, sacrifices something.

The prophetic sense of the new is manifested by the life of Jesus; he no longer tolerates any separation between worship and charity. This is the great theme of the prophets. Isaiah, Jeremiah and Ezekiel protested against men whose acts of worship did not lead to a transformation of social life, to better interpersonal relationships. All the prophets insisted on the fact that one who adores the living God, the true Creator of all men, should be moved by mercy. It is in the Sermon on the Mount that Jesus teaches us the Our Father and makes clear that a man is the greatest of liars who says: 'Our Father," and does not also say by his life "my brethren," because all men are true sons of God. The Our Father intimately links the Father of all men with the brotherly relationship of neighbor.

The prophetic mission of Christ is all the more evident in that he does not belong to the hereditary priestly caste. He is not a son of Aaron, does not belong to the tribe of Levi and receives no priestly allowance. He is the true priest according to the order of Melchizedek, a priest who did not belong to the status quo. In the Sermon on the Mount, Jesus castigates those who employ religion for purposes of human prestige or social status. In fact, Jesus is a priest but in the prophetic sense and, as we shall see, in the most profound, nonviolent sense of the victory of love which even entails the sacrifice of one's own life. Although Jesus was not a social reformer, in the Sermon on the Mount he teaches us to have a new attitude toward earthly possessions. He shows that material goods are gifts of the one Father and if we are to rejoice in them it is by making them means of love, by using these gifts of God in the service of others and not as the mammon of man who wants to possess them selfishly. If the Christian reflects, he soon realizes that everything is a gift and manifestation of the love of the one Father, and he will transform God's bounties into the language of fraternal love and will do so with that complete freedom which is diametrically opposed to the status quo. "So do not be anxious about tomorrow; tomorrow will look after itself" (Matt. 6:34). So far then as the use of earthly goods is concerned, we are called to do every day whatever good can be done. This does not mean that new times will not call for new clarifications of the rule, or even new forms of long-term planning, but it does mean that man must be completely free in this respect. The disciple of Christ can never allow himself to be enslaved by earthly preoccupations.

The Dynamism of Nonviolence

To understand fully the meaning of nonviolence, which we can define as the energies gathered by love and nourished by faith, hope and charity, we must bear in mind that the

Gospel morality is something dynamic. The whole perspective of the Sermon on the Mount is that to be a Christian means to be progressive. Its whole message goes beyond a merely static, prohibitive idea of the law: "it is said." Jesus is revolted by self-satisfaction and any form of lukewarm acquiescence. The law proclaimed on the Mount of Beatitudes is a law of joy. "The joy of the Lord is our strength," says the book of Nehemiah (chapter 8, verse 11) in the Old Testament. In the Sermon on the Mount, Jesus sets in motion the whole of man, speaking to his heart, to his mind, to his will, so that the whole man, man in his entirety, will let himself be guided by the love of God. It becomes clear therefore that this new law "I say to you" is no bulwark canonizing the status quo, no policing of existing social structures. The policeman can never become the ideal of the religious man, the symbol of the new order. The key to what nonviolence really means is obviously the full manifestation of the heavenly Father and of all his works in Christ. God the Father shows his perfection precisely in his nonviolent, merciful and absolutely active love of men who have offended him, in his love of enemies. Christ dies for men who have offended God through sin.

The Sermon on the Mount should be read in the light of the Paschal Mystery, but in the same light we should also view all the facts of creation. God gives the light of the sun, the heat of the sun, and rain to the good and the bad alike to convert them, to conquer them by love. The Sermon on the Mount is presented by Matthew as the dynamic law of the new covenant, as opposed to the rather static law of Sinai where Moses, the supreme lawgiver, remained aloof from the people, standing alone on a mountain. St. Matthew contrasts this with the new reality, that of the new lawgiver, the authority of the Emmanuel who mixes with the crowd and speaks when surrounded by his disciples. Jesus speaks with the authority of his love; therefore, with full authority. In this context Jesus proclaims the joy and gentleness of the man of invincible love. To him has been given the new land and the "shalom" which the Old Testament has already described as a gift from heaven, but a gift that man gathers only if he is devoted to an order of love and peace. If man does not devote himself to peace, he actually refuses to receive the messianic peace because when man truly receives peace, he is transformed and becomes a dynamic presence of the gift of God, a sacrament, a visible sign of peace.

Nonviolence, the Fruit of Conversion

It is very important for us to understand clearly what is meant by the idea of repentance in the Sermon on the Mount. There can be no new birth without repentance. Man must see that his being is contaminated by evil, or as the non-believing humanist Erich Fromm puts it, "Woe to the man who does not have the strength and the courage to confront the obscure forces behind his back." Woe to the man who seeks to escape, who does not want to come to grips with reality, even the obscure reality of his past life, who does not know how to transform his past by means of repentance, who, as Scripture shows us, is always overly self-confident and at the same time plagued by security-insecurity complexes.

The man who devotes himself to nonviolence and nonviolent means knows that he will always remain a vulnerable man. Only God, because he is love, cannot be contaminated by evil. That is why St. Paul warns us not to be guided by vindictive justice because man can too easily be tainted by it. Nonviolence is the richness, the energy, the invincible strength of those who love. Only a great and humble love that hopes all can put up with the difficulties, the opposition and the insults without becoming bitter. When rancor takes possession of man, he has already lost a good part of his energies; he can no longer promote the revolution of love.

The Dynamic Norm and Casuistry

The Sermon on the Mount does not provide us with concrete solutions such as are found in classical textbooks but it obviously tries to get our attention by the use of imagery and colorful language. "If anyone slaps you on the right cheek, turn and offer him your left." When the servant of the high priest struck Jesus on the right cheek, he did not tell him to hit him also on the left cheek. Rather, with all the disciplined energies of love, he reproved him: "If I have done evil show me, if I have not done evil why do you strike me?" We must not draw simplistic conclusions. Gentleness is not a weak virtue.

Once during the last war when I was serving in the medical corps, one of my colleagues said harsh words about the church and religion; in fact, he attacked it openly in the presence of an officer. Everybody there was aware of my presence and priestly status. The severe look on my face, a truly nonviolent expression, told the officer (a nonbeliever, a Nazi): "If you have any sense of honor, I expect you to make this man apologize. Tomorrow if you are hit, I will have to assist you. Today you are insulting me to my face because of my religion. This man should apologize and you should make him do so." My comrade had to apologize and he was compelled to do so by one who did not believe in any religion. If we are timid, if we are afraid that there may be unpleasant consequences, even, or perhaps especially, in our ecclesiastical relations, we shall always be treated badly. If, on the other hand, we show strength, we can expect to be listened to and respected. Whatever must be said, however, must be said properly, without hatred, with firmness and decision. Part of being nonviolent is the ability to speak with firmness, with energy, and with courage especially to those who have it in their power to harm us. Not all cases can be settled in the same way; some must be resolved according to circumstances, but we must know what the basic attitude is, what the goal is, and what the appropriate means are.

As I mentioned earlier, I think that the attempted assassination of Hitler on July 20, 1944, was justified, but not the prolonged delay. It should not have been inspired by rancor. Father Delp, a Jesuit priest who was killed shortly after this attempt, and even the generals who planned the assassination acted without rancor and with a sense of responsibility for a nation and for other nations exposed to the extreme danger of destruction. Dietrich Bonhoeffer, the famous Protestant theologian implicated in this attempt, was a pacifist, a preacher of nonviolence. These are extreme cases about which there may be discussion and perhaps we can even arrive at a measure of agreement, but we must be careful not to set up a new kind of legalism. If it is a question of suffering, of the unheard-of sufferings of millions of people, if we have exhausted all other nonviolent means, we cannot count the life of a single criminal. So can we also discuss the death penalty. Personally, I expressed myself very clearly on these issues twenty years ago when I voted for the abolition of the death penalty, particularly in a state which had a terrible record for killing.

Another example will serve to illustrate the limits and at the same time the spirit of nonviolence: a Jesuit student tried to help persons wounded during the demonstrations at the University of Rome in 1968. As he was doing so, a policeman took him aside and they talked peacefully. He was a rather calm individual. Another policeman soon came up and hit him on the head; the young Jesuit had to spend three weeks in the hospital and pay for it himself. Certainly, the latter policeman indulged in an act of violence; he had no motive to justify the blow on the head. It was an example of aggressiveness, of undisciplined recourse to force on the part of one who had allowed himself to be infected by violence.

I feel that we should take a closer look at our jails and our whole system of "vindictive justice": is the latter not too often infected by a kind of vindictive violence which makes us unable to love the persons involved? The violence of the system is one of the reasons why so many criminals try to escape from jail.

Nonviolence is disciplined force invoked for the protection of others. Violence, on the other hand, is always an undisciplined outburst, an expression of rancor. The above policeman was not prepared psychologically for nonviolence; he had not been educated to methods of self-discipline. We must distinguish disciplined force from an expression of passion, rancor, or violence. Thus, I would make this sharp distinction between a disciplined use of force when it is necessary to protect the innocent, and violence as the undisciplined and unjust use of force. When we do use force to restrain an aggressor or unjust man within limits or in order to overcome an unjust status quo, we must always bear in mind two conditions: (1) we must use the minimum of coercive force with a maximum of concern for justice; (2) we must not become infected by the violence of others. If a state employs the maximum of force with a minimum of concern for social reform it has failed. I can cite the example of Brazil, which, before becoming a complete dictatorship, devoted 49 percent of the federal taxes to the army and 9 percent to education. This represents an incredible disproportion. The nation having the greatest human potential has need of the best in the way of professional and human education.

We see a similar disproportion in the case of so many

moral theologians who devote up to 95 percent of their energies to the casuistry of the minimum, to controls and restraints, and perhaps 5 percent to promoting the ideal. In nonviolence, even in the use of force, there must always be the following disproportion: a maximum of concern for man, a maximal expression of true love even for those who resist us, coupled with a minimum of coercive force, the absolute minimum necessary. It is precisely this want of disproportion that is disturbing the world today.

Violence is not only a reality on the level of social, national, and international relations; it is above all a feature of the man who does not believe in the force of love. We frequently find among conservatives in the church today that they do not believe in the saving force of love and this to the point of saying: "It is better not to speak of love; we should rather speak only of duties and proper controls with regard to its fulfillment." Violence can also be expressed in sarcasm or irony depending upon the circumstances. The Old Testament prophets who were nonviolent (perhaps with the exception of Elias, a rather violent prophet) sometimes employed sarcasm but never against those who were weak. Jesus himself uses sarcasm as well as irony in the parable of the Samaritan in this way; his barbs were directed against the powerful, violent class of the Pharisees and priests. A man is lying in his blood; a priest comes along, sees him, and passes him by. A Levite comes along, sees him, and also passes him by. Here we have a searing sarcasm, a word that pierces the heart, but it is clear that Jesus is driven by love to convert and to save men. It is clear from the context that the story is an ultimate passionate effort on his part to overcome the false security and self-sufficiency of the Pharisees.

Will Nonviolence Triumph?

Speaking of the Sermon on the Mount, we must first of all notice that it is Christ who is at the center of the picture. He has overcome evil by love. But even with respect to Christ, we can raise the question: Will nonviolence triumph? Is nonviolence enough? We may say, first of all, that Christ, the great nonviolent One, was sacrificed and was overcome by darkness, but it was precisely at this moment that he celebrated his victory: "Father, forgive them for they do not know what they are doing." Similarly Stephen, the prophet deacon, who with a pointed sermon against the Establishment conquered at the very moment when he was being stoned, saying: "Lord Jesus, do not impute this sin to them." It is the victory of love; and this is the difference between immediate success and true victory.

To Peter, who hoped for a Messiah who would triumph through violence, Jesus said clearly: "Put up your sword. All who take the sword die by the sword" (Matt. 26:52). Therefore, the power of the sword, even if it conquers temporarily, is already a sign that man himself has been overcome by evil; he has allowed himself to be contaminated. It is precisely here that the great efforts and example of Martin Luther King, of Gandhi, and of men who have always shown a great love toward their opponents, have relevance. Dr. King always told his Negro followers: "The whites are perhaps sicker than we are. We can help them to get well only if we display a disciplined love."

An Italian priest in the United States, Father Groppi of Milwaukee, has also become famous in this sense because of his nonviolent and disciplined protests against an unjust system that excludes Negroes from the more prosperous sectors of cities. He has been able to influence his Negro friends without imposing himself as their leader. In fact, he has succeeded in getting all these Negroes to protest in a disciplined way. Even when the Catholic whites of Polish or German descent insulted them violently, the Negro friends of Father Groppi have morally triumphed by showing a discipline that came from their belief that their opponents were sick men who had to employ such brutal means to defend their status quo.

Such courageous deeds spring from an aroused conscience. The nonviolent have a provocative force; I refrain from using "violence" because we must show respect for the meaning of terms. Active nonviolence is a disconcerting force that can overcome the false security, the self-sufficiency of the defenders of the unjust status quo. True nonviolence is a courageous force that profoundly shakes the sense of security.

After two millennia of Christianity, we may finally ask why nonviolence has not been more successful. The answer entails a humiliating examination of conscience for all Christians. We have placed too much confidence in violence and too little confidence in love: this is our real weakness.

We have defined the dogmas of faith, but we have not clearly seen the immense dynamism of faith itself. If one says: "Father of Our Lord Jesus Christ," he says this only *in truth* if he believes that God is Father of all men, that he is love and that God conquers by means of love. We have not sufficiently inculcated the strength of pacifism; we have frequently equated nonviolence with laziness: withdrawing, escaping, remaining aloof and quiet. We cannot call a Christian nonviolent who is not interested in or does not see that a new relationship with God immediately means a new relationship with neighbor; that a relationship with God the Father of all is not sincere without an active concern for a more just world. Part of this responsibility rests with our moral theologians. Perhaps what I am saying here will mean another open letter from some monsignor such as happened to me some three years ago. I am referring to the static morality of recent centuries, a morality too concerned with the meticulous control of others, with artificial distinctions between mortal and venial sins; in short, a very superficial morality that has contributed to this lack of energy. Only a dynamic morality which places the accent on the seven-times repeated "I say to you . . . ," which points the direction we are to take—only such a morality can overcome the violence of the unjust status quo, the violence of conservative nationalism, of religious traditionalism, etc., which always occasions new undisciplined explosions on the part of the opposition.

We must protest against that violence that in the name of lofty concepts, such as authority and public order, defends an absolutely unjust status quo because it exists only for the

III

Man's Quest for Freedom in Community

The greatest liberating power is that of love: love in its fullness as social and interpersonal relationships, love growing in its articulation with justice, wisdom, valor, and temperance. Man imprisoned in his own ego remains underdeveloped, a slave to narrowness and pettiness. The human person finds himself only in encounter with the Thou, in genuine human relationships respecting and fostering the freedom of all.

Love itself is threatened by the desire to dominate the other person. Love and freedom are possible only in mutual respect, in mutual giving and receiving on all human levels.

In its very first pages, the Bible describes sin as disregard for God, loss of the communion of love with God, and disregard for the other person. The immediate result of sin is domination of man over woman.

Historically, the disturbed balance of liberty between man and woman seems to have been first in the direction of matriarchalism. When woman invented horticulture, she often took advantage of her position and tried to possess man (the husband and the children) as she possessed the garden and the cottage; of course, she took care of man as she took care of the herbs and trees. She "ate of the fruit" of domination and thus she contaminated man, who was equally if not more eager to take advantage of his economic and cultural advantages: organized hunting in the totem cultures, and the more highly organized agriculture once man had domesticated the animals. "Your husband will lord it over you" (Gen. 3:16).

Whenever the relationships between husband and wife are disturbed by a system of inequality and domination, the relationships between parents and children will also be disturbed. Education, therefore, consists more in training for obedience than in training for the proper use of freedom. Every system of domination manifests a certain immaturity, a lack of the capacity to love another out of mutual respect; such a system tends to keep people immature.

Paternalism as Alienation

A family system in which domination is accepted as a "natural right" (cf: *Casti Connubii!*) taints all other social relationships. A male-centered society can neither truly appreciate nor fully realize human respect and freedom. There is an inherent interdependence between the family structure and all other social relationships and structures.

Where excessive patriarchalism is a well-established and unquestionably accepted family pattern, the whole human person will reflect the same basic structure. It is then that even God appears as lording it over man rather than sharing his love with man. In the worst of situations, the image of God intimidates man (scrupulosity, etc.) when the father as authority-figure intimidates the wife and children. In the best of situations, where the forceful and unquestioned father-authority grants a kind of security, religiosity and morality will focus chiefly on security and on the maintenance of the status quo.

The great proprietors in many Latin American societies, in the agricultural and industrial modern economy, are characterized by the same brand of paternalism as corresponds to the male-centered, strong patriarchal family structure. The paternalist expects gratitude and submission since he supplies the needs of the people. He is convinced that he knows better and more than those under his control. He promises security and defends the status quo for security's sake. The whole system, of course, is based on the conviction that the paternalistic mode of domination is good, but it soon degenerates into a brutal exploitation marked by no evident concern for those exploited.

Patriarchalism-Paternalism-Centralism and Individualism

A strongly developed patriarchalism and widespread paternalism in the cultural, economic and social sphere will inevitably tend to promote centralism. A despotic patriarchalism overemphasizes the dependent relationship of all family members on the head of the family. The overtone is that of obedience to the one who issues all orders. The other intrafamily relationships of necessity remain in the embryonic stage of development, or else they atrophy. The paternalistic outlook in the cultural and socioeconomic sphere fails to encourage well-developed forms of sharing and mutual responsibility, save those forms which promote the observance of existing regulations or paternalistic precepts. It follows that under a paternalistic regime a certain individualism will develop naturally. The individualistic behavior, however, will be rewarded and ever better sustained by a system of strict laws and controls.

Paternalism and centralism realize that the preservation of the existing order and power will be easier if small groups and individuals seek their own security and advantages independently without association with others, without subsidiarity, in total dependence on the protecting authority. The typical paternalist, for example, has always been opposed to any form of labor unionism.

Another example would be the centralism of the Western Latin Church, which for centuries reflected the prevailing centralism of the larger civic society. The bishop in one diocese had little if any direct relationship to other bishops and dioceses. Security emanated from the central government in Rome. The same held true concerning the relationship of parish to diocese, with a consequent marked group egotism at both levels, a group egotism corresponding closely to the basic individualism. Legalism is the accepted medium of the whole system, which promotes—as a kind of compensation—this kind of individualism while protecting the status quo through centralism.

Interaction of Social Structures and the Community of Faith

Christ enriches the world with the liberating power of a love that is humble, i.e., devoid of all types of domineeringness, and an exercise of authority characterized by service and interested in fostering maturity, initiative, and brotherhood. "In the world, kings lord it over their subjects; and those in authority are called their country's 'Benefactors.' Not so with you; on the contrary, the highest among you must bear himself like the youngest, the chief of you like a servant. . . . Yet here am I among you like a servant" (Luke 22:25–27). Christ does not want a bare system of external rules and blind obedience; he wants mature Christians who act with deep insight and in a spirit of solidarity. "I call you servants no longer; a servant does not know what his master is about. I have called you friends, because I have disclosed to you everything that I heard from my Father" (John

15:15). Since then, the gospel of redeeming love and the new concept and new shape of authority in the community of the disciples of Christ has been a ferment in society.

The church as a social institution is also exposed to the "old leaven" of a patriarchal, paternalistic and domineering society. As the Church of the Word Incarnate, she can and must somehow adjust herself and her structures to the existing society, guarding herself always against the danger of contamination. Her being in the world must be dynamic and prophetic, forever questioning the status quo and striving ever toward conversion on all levels. Should the church be self-complacent and cling rigidly to inherited structures, she would dangerously alienate herself from her mission. The danger is all the greater if she becomes entangled in "sacred alliances" with the dominating powers of paternalism and dictatorship, whose chief concern is the maintenance of an unjust status quo. At a time when our whole society and culture are undergoing deep transformations, it becomes more and more unjust for any social unit to cling to the status quo. In his now famous interview of May 1969, Cardinal Suenens put his finger on the problem: What kind of image does the church convey with its present system of nuncios and apostolic delegates accredited to conservative governments and acting as the principal liaison between the Vicar of Christ and the local bishops?

Only to the extent that the church gratefully and humbly accepts the prophetic protest and protests against her own outmoded, immobile structures and attitudes can she be the leaven for a humanity longing for greater freedom. The church must herself yearn for the liberty of the sons and daughters of God in the totality of her life. To think that the freedom of God's children can exist in man's innermost being alone without communicating itself to the whole of man's life is already a sign of alienation, of enslavement by an establishment that thinks in terms of status quo structures.

Such an attitude is reflected, for example, by movements (immobile "movements") for the preservation of "family, tradition and property," understood as the preservation of the patriarchal concept of family and society and the present distribution of property. Of course, such organizations as *"Pro familia, tradição, propriedade"* (in Brazil headed by a traditionalist bishop), as well as the John Birch Society, can have a healthy function but only to the extent that they serve to unmask for all to see the connection between family-patriarchalism or church-paternalism, traditionalism and concern for the status quo as regards the distribution of wealth and power.

Only then to the extent that the church purifies herself by the painful process of protest, self-criticism, self-denial and reform will her voice be credible in a society yearning for liberation. The community of faith is more influential by means of presence and witness, by unmistakable interdependence (where the stronger and more authentic self-manifestation speaks for itself), than by means of a social doctrine which does not reflect itself in the church's own life and structures.

In this sense, the implementation and doctrinal development of collegiality within the whole life of the church is a necessary condition for the effective teaching of the basic principle of subsidiarity in the modern world.

Subsidiarity

Two key characteristics of a society of truly free persons are the principles of subsidiarity and solidarity. In modern society especially, subsidiarity is the very opposite of paternalism and centralism, whereas solidarity represents the victory over individualism and group egotism. As a dynamic process of liberating efforts, subsidiarity starts "from below" and encourages, fosters, and, where needed, coordinates "from above" while gradually blurring the lines of "below" and "above," at least as regards useless privileges. Freedom exists in the concert of responsible persons and communities who encourage the maximum of initiative with the maximum of responsibility for the whole of society. Subsidiarity means shared responsibility and, to some extent, shared authority. The higher authority and the larger group should respect, foster and protect the functions that are properly those of the individual person or smaller group. Both should be encouraged: personal initiative and group initiative in view of the common good. When extraordinary difficulties forcibly curtail the exercise of the normal functions and rights of persons or groups, these functions and rights "should be restored as quickly as possible after the emergency passes."[1]

[1] *Gaudium et spes*, Art. 75.

All the relationships among the various communities and authorities should be marked by the readiness to contribute to the greatest possible liberty and the best possible discharge of responsibility at all levels. Individuals and small groups should only accept (and be offered) assistance which does not suffocate but rather stimulates and sets free initiative and responsibility.

The extraordinary Synod of Bishops in Rome, in October 1969, was an effort to apply these principles more visibly and effectively to the basic structures of the church. At stake is the prophetic role of the church in the modern world.

Progress in Freedom and Education

In a society where only a few had access to higher learning, paternalism was appreciated as an expression of concern for and service toward weaker persons. Family patriarchalism was also characterized by an educational gap between man and woman. The wife who was trained only for household duties and child rearing willingly accepted a moderate patriarchal authority on the part of her husband, gladly renouncing any claim to represent her own or the family's rights outside the family.

Our highly scientific, technological age, by contrast, characterized as it is by mass-communications media and the general desire to share in learning and culture, cannot put up with the older forms of paternalism and centralism any longer. Where possibilities exist for sharing the goods of cultural progress and social responsibility more equally, the older forms of inequality are seen as strikingly unjust and severely judged as obstacles to greater freedom.

If society wants to avoid unnecessary tensions and conflicts, freedom has to begin simultaneously on all levels. I greatly favor equal opportunities for all women and men. This should quickly have a bearing on family structures. The simultaneous effort to curb prostitution and similar forms of the exploitation of women must be organized and coordinated with positive efforts to foster and promote the new role and equal dignity of woman. The partnership family is posited as an essential condition for the liberation of man and woman from the base desire to dominate each other.

Human life should be conceived as a system of interdependencies, the most decisive being the interdependence of family and other social entities: the community of faith (religion) and social life (including family and marriage). It is imperative, therefore, to direct all efforts toward overcoming all forms of alienation and domination in the areas of the family and religion. Toward this end, modern means of communication and mass education can be most important instruments. There is no doubt that they can also be used to promote new forms of slavery, but they should be used as instruments of liberation. For instance, if all believers enjoy a high level of education and at the same time have a good knowledge of the faith, the relationship between clergy and laity can change in the direction of a greater sharing of learning and responsibility. As a consequence, the relationships between "higher" and "lower" clergy will also change.

No Romantic I-Thou Island

In the past, man spent more than 80 percent of his time within the patriarchal family and within social structures modeled on that of the family. Today, modern man spends more than 80 percent of his waking hours outside the family circle, in a highly organized and "impersonal" social and economic world. As a necessary reaction to this depersonalizing environment, man feels a greater need for the intimate relationships of marriage, family life and friendship. Modern personalism's emphasis on the I-Thou relationship reflects this new psychological and sociological reality. Society will surely lose its "soul," its human quality, if man does not cultivate genuine personal relationships in marriage, the family, in friendships and in small communities. The profound transformation of all of society today calls for a totally new balance between intimate personal relationships on the one hand and life in the socioeconomic sphere on the other; this is an absolute condition for man's liberation.

Two different "romantic" temptations are likely to occur in this respect. The first would be building a romantic "I-Thou Island" without a liberating commitment to the claims of economic, social and cultural life. The icy-cold relationships of the socioeconomic sphere compel man to seek warm relationships and fulfillment almost exclusively in friendships or marriage and the family. The I-Thou relationship becomes the island on which he wants to dwell if he is to find a personal life-style and happiness. Socioeconomic life then becomes the "other world" into which he penetrates solely for the purpose of obtaining the necessities for his "real life" in marriage and the family. Psychologically, there is a dichotomy between the world of love and the world of justice or unjust economic structures. The warmth and respect characteristic of the personal relationships in the small world do not extend to the social and economic sphere. A person's interests and commitments are almost totally confined to intimate-group life. It follows that this kind of friendship can degenerate into a small-group egotism comprising two or three persons. In any case, the world would not become more humanized if all the dyads and triads acted that way. In this case the family and all these inhabitants of the "I-Thou Islands" would be creating stifling, suffocating social environments on which they would turn their backs. But are not the powers behind our backs often the most dangerous to our freedom?

The other form of "romanticism" is the archaic concept of economy and society as an "extension" of the patriarchal family. This unrealistic concept underlies the many forms of paternalism of the great landowners and the so-called family enterprises of the early phases of capitalism. The concept of property is linked to the immediate family. In the name of "family, tradition and property" all new forms of shared property and shared responsibility are suspect and declared communistic or Marxist. Some Catholic moralists of the traditional school (e.g., C. Ermecke) went so far as to propose an ethic of socioeconomic life under the heading of "familiarism."

In a religious sense we can refer to mankind as "the family of God," since we all have God as our Creator, Redeemer and Father, but we must recognize the profound differences in personal relationships between the family and modern organizations, both on an organizational and on a psychological level. I am not playing down the transitional elements of intermediate types of communities. There are definitely similarities between a family-community and cultural, social, economic relationships and structures. But woe to those people who plan their family life according to the model of a bank or seek the same kind of relationships in banking matters as in the intimate family circle.

The I-Thou relationship must not be confused with an institutional structure or contractual obligations. Despite Joseph Fletcher, in view of our modern life and even more so because of it, we must distinguish between love and justice. Love and justice are interrelated but they are not identical. Love has differing wavelengths, starting from the most intimate relationships in marriage and family life or a religious community and extending to big corporations and international bodies.

A realistic approach distinguishes sharply between love and justice, but one's perspective should be integrative. For a healthy development of persons and interpersonal relationships, for a wholesome reciprocation of love, there can be no dichotomy between the I-Thou community and broader social life. The human person is molded by the totality of his environment and, above all, by his attitude toward this whole environment. For man to remain truly a person, he must be open to the other and to the world in which men live. Unless man continually tries to shape and reshape his world, his relationships and the structures which condition or change them, he will never attain the full dimensions of freedom.

The good of freedom expresses itself in many forms and on many levels, but in the final analysis it is the good of an undivided freedom. Mankind has to strive toward that ever greater freedom befitting man's nature and this, by means of personal initiative and common effort. Man contributes to the undivided freedom of all by a wise commitment to his neighbor and to society. At the same time, the human person constantly experiences the extent to which he is indebted to the community and society or is threatened by it.

Solidarity and Nonviolence

In the last analysis, liberation means the full development of all the energies of love and justice and the human environment in which these energies of love can find a better development. Such development aims to have the world around us both encourage and foster the free commitment, the constant effort to set free the energies of love.

The freedom of the human person, of communities and societies is not something gained once and for all. Freedom has to be won and deepened by a constant struggle against the radiations of frustration and slavery that come from the unfree world around us, particularly from persons who do not know what genuine freedom is and therefore fail to commit themselves to the undivided good of freedom.

Genuine freedom cannot be enforced by means diametrically opposed to true freedom, namely, the freedom to develop all the energies of love and justice. Freedom and liberation for freedom can only be acquired by the right use of freedom expressed in love and solidarity.

Nonviolence, understood as an active commitment to freedom and as the art of collecting one's love-energies for the sake of freedom in justice, is an expression of solidarity. Nonviolence arises from the deep conviction of human solidarity. We are truly becoming free if we evince concern for the freedom of all and justice for all.

Nonviolence does not imply passivity or lack of fortitude. Neither is it a cowardly acceptance of the status quo with its attendant impediments to freedom. Nonviolence is at the same time an active and wise commitment to freedom in love and justice.

The Christian conviction of the solidarity of all before God, Creator and Redeemer of all men, enables the Christian to love his enemies, to show his concern for the "liberation" of oppressors and tyrants as well as the oppressed. Since the ultimate goal lies in the liberation of all the energies of love for the full realization of every human person in all his capabilities, the means and methods toward this end must be such as to express this love and contribute

IV

Toward Maturity

All Christians are called to holiness, to the fullness of love. This calling implies a life of growth toward full Christian maturity—maturity of conscience, maturity in the knowledge of Christ, of God, of fellowman, of self and of the world—in order to love God and neighbor with all our strength and with full knowledge of what we are doing.

In its own deep, simple way, Holy Scripture speaks of the universality of this vocation: "May you be strong to grasp, with all God's people, what is the breadth and length and height and depth of the love of Christ, and to know it, though it is beyond knowledge. So shall you attain the fullness of being, the fullness to which God calls you" (Eph. 3:17-19). The emphasis is on "all God's people."

The great biblical message that everybody is called to maturity was first proclaimed in a world that was divided into a small elite group and a great mass of slaves. The ancient world divided mankind into two classes—the few who had the opportunity to achieve maturity and the many who were kept in such conditions that they could not achieve it. This is reflected in the ethics of the Stoics as well as in the ideologies of many religious "monopolies." Similarly, the philosophy of Plato, Aristotle and many others was for the few; it had little meaning for the masses. Even the most "religious" people in Israel, the Pharisees, considered the multitudes cursed because they could not obtain full knowledge of the law.

Into that unequal world came the message that *all* of God's people, not only the few, are called to a mature character, to a deep knowledge of God and his designs. On Pentecost, after the Holy Spirit had come upon the apostles and those gathered around them, St. Peter's first words were: "God says 'I will pour out upon everyone a portion of my spirit; your sons and daughters shall prophesy, even slaves, both men and women, will prophesy'" (Acts 2:70).

We must visualize these words in the context of the times. Women were not admitted to the synagogue when the Book of the Covenant was read. The husband could choose to tell his wife and daughter only what he considered within the reach of their intelligence. Now comes the word that the Spirit is poured upon all without exception, men and women, even slave girls.

The theme of Christian maturity is always actual, always existential. It addresses everyone regardless of social or cultural background, calling all to a knowledge of God and to active participation in his design. This is particularly relevant at a time when totally new responsibilities, opportunities and dangers confront mankind.

In past centuries, conditions were often such as to make higher culture and learning the prerogative of a very small group. In the early Middle Ages, for instance, higher learning became practically the monopoly of the clergy, although the situation was a necessary development; at that time, the clergy rendered true service to mankind. In the Dark Ages of the Norman invasions, when almost all the centers of learning and culture were destroyed, the clergy preserved learning in the schools gathered around the cathedrals and in the monasteries. However, in time they pretended that learning and culture were their particular preserve.

Traces of this attitude lingered even into the church of the nineteenth century. One example will illustrate the tendency: Dom Guéranger, who was a great liturgical scholar in his day, objected to the translation of the mass into French because he considered it an affront to the clergy and monks since mother church, in her wisdom, had reserved the words of the canon of the mass to priests and monks who knew Latin. He felt slighted by the prospect of having the canon profaned by translating it for "unlearned servant-maids and simple workers." This was truly representative of an immature aristocratic outlook. These ecclesiastical aristocrats had evidently not matured themselves in the sense of the Gospel, since they were not devoting their energies to the task of bringing all "to the full stature of Christ."

The situation is different today. Over the centuries the

laity has increasingly taken over the leadership in science and culture, although not without occasional crises: the Galileo case was one such. Higher learning is now open to all, to women as well as to men. Of course, some clergymen blended their voices with those of the laity protesting the admittance of women to colleges and universities. There are always groups and individuals who would dam up the stream of life if they could.

The pace of change has been accelerating lately. More than one third of North American youth now receive a college education, and even those who do not enjoy this privilege have unprecedented opportunities to share in the cultural richness of life through mass-communications media. Of itself, this does not guarantee the future of man's liberty and dignity; this can only be ensured by a fuller participation in the responsibilities of economic, cultural, social and political life. It does, however, provide a broadened base for the continual renewal of structures, for the formation of public opinion and the creation of new attitudes toward life. We see the youth of today openly protesting against forms of establishment and authority that block their sharing in responsibility and hinder the development of more mature personal relationships.

In this frame of reference, many concepts have to be seen in a different light; obedience is but one example. According to the old monolithic closed culture pattern, it was best for the masses to adopt an attitude of passive, even blind obedience toward the better-informed ruling classes. A certain amount of stability and order was maintained and preserved by this way of thinking.

There was a time when the church thought its chief task was to watch over people. The pastor, because of his influence in the parish community, could impose a standard of behavior on all. Today, most Christians come under a pastor's influence for only minutes weekly, while the rest of their time is spent coping with the impact of the secular environment. If young people in the family and in church learn only to be "good" by being "obedient" and by conforming, then in another environment they will slavishly conform to voices or pressures around them. They will be ill-equipped to discern values and to act according to their own consciences.

Christians are called to be the "salt of the earth and the light of the world." As to the dimensions of the vocation, St. Paul writes: "So shall we all attain to the unity inherent in our faith and our knowledge of the Son of God, to a mature character measured by nothing less than the full stature of Christ" (Eph. 4:13). Here we have the final definition of Christian maturity: "a character measured by nothing less than the full stature of Christ." Christians can fulfill this role only to the extent that they understand the meaning of man, have deep faith, have formed and informed consciences, and have the courage to take initiatives. Today more than ever, Christians must strive for increased proficiency in the social sciences, in politics, in economics and in the arts, as well as in religion. Only then will they be preparing themselves for a mature relationship to their fellowmen and their environment.

Christian maturity in character, love and knowledge is a

gift of the Holy Spirit; included are all the God-given natural qualities of each individual. Maturity is not automatically produced by the social environment, but the person who acknowledges the tremendous impact of the environment on behavior can be a leaven transforming our whole culture and social life. In view of our own vocation as persons and of our responsibility for the world around us, we are obliged to strive toward an ever greater maturity "measured by nothing less than the full stature of Christ." In an effort to present an integrated picture of the mature Christian personality in the light of the special needs and circumstances of our age, I call attention to some specific points.

Open-mindedness

(1) *Open-mindedness,* maturity's first prerequisite, is that keen and constant awareness of the presence of the living God and of relationships to our neighbor. We live in their presence, aware of God's holiness and the uniqueness, individuality and social character of our brothers and sisters. To come to have an understanding and respect for them is totally different from analyzing them or imposing on them abstract ideas and principles.

It should not surprise us that Gabriel Marcel considers this so-called "abstraction" one of the most dangerous causes of war. Essentially, he claims that one must transform individuals into abstractions if one is to wage war against them:

As soon as anyone claims of me that I commit myself to a warlike action against other human beings, whom I must as a consequence of my commitment be ready to destroy, it is very necessary from the point of view of those who are influencing me that I lose all awareness of the individual reality of the being whom I may be led to destroy. In order to transform him into a mere impersonal target, it is absolutely necessary to convert him into an abstraction: *the* Communist, *the* anti-Fascist, *the* Fascist, and so on . . .[1]

If we are to love an enemy, a friend, a prisoner, a Communist, a Vietcong, or another Christian, it must be by individualizing and personalizing him.

The mature Christian knows what enters into a true I-Thou-We relationship and his primary concern is to live fully on this level. He strives always toward a deeper knowledge of God and of man through a greater appreciation of Christ who is the God-man. An existential knowledge of the real needs of man is very different from an abstract knowledge by which people so often coldly "judge" and discriminate.

Genuine Communication and Respect

(2) Maturity reveals itself especially in *genuine communication,* in deep *respect* for the other, coupled with a healthy

---

[1] Gabriel Marcel, *Man Against Mass Society* (Gateway, 1952), pp. 157-158.

self-respect. Respect for the Thou and for the self is our response to God who calls each of us by name and all of us together to a communion of saints. Genuine communication is an expression of respect. The respectful person can listen to others and appreciate all the good in them.

The Capacity to Reciprocate Love

(3) A person's maturity can be measured by his or her *capacity to love* in mutual respect, with joyous appreciation of the opportunities to be of service and by the *capacity to receive love in gratitude and joy.* A mature person knows how to express love on the different levels of his relationships: family, friends, community, organization, society. Not only does he enjoy a clear and deep discernment of values but he has ordered them according to a sound hierarchy of values. To him values, ideals and principles are not abstract ideas but the message of a loving God. He knows that he can communicate love in the service of man only when he adheres to authentic values out of deep respect for the dignity of each individual person.

Action Follows Knowledge

(4) Knowledge alone, regardless of its depth or scope, does not make for maturity. It is only when a person *acts upon his knowledge,* when he strives toward more light and full

implementation of the knowledge he has, placing it in the service of the common good, that the sincerity and integrity of the person are preserved and deepened.

Judgments of Conscience

(5) One of the major differentials serving to distinguish mature from immature people is the *breadth* or narrowness of their focus in making *judgments of conscience*. The immature Christian focuses on the boundary line: Is this a sin or not? Is it a mortal or a venial sin? The eyes of conscience consistently fail to see the magnificent scope of the whole Christian vocation; he raises no questions about it. The mature Christian, on the other hand, seeks the boundaries only in the perspective of growth toward greater fullness of personal life. He makes his judgments in confrontation with the living God, the Gospel, assessing the gifts he has received from God and capitalizing on the present opportunities to strengthen the bonds of love and justice among people. He looks to God, asking: "How can I please you? What can I render you for all you have given me?" He arrives at an integrated view of the Gospel and morality, of the gifts of God and his responsibilities, by looking to the real needs of men and finding there vital principles to guide him in genuine expressions of love.

With reference to the "Dignity of the Moral Conscience," Article 16 of the *Constitution on the Church in the Modern World* says: "In the depths of his conscience man detects a law which he does not impose upon himself but which holds him to obedience. Always summoning him to love good and avoid evil, the voice of conscience can, when necessary, speak to him specifically: do this, shun that. For man has in his heart a law written by God. To obey it is the very dignity of man; according to it he will be judged.

"Conscience is the most secret core and sanctuary of a man. There he is alone with God, whose voice echoes in his depths. In a wonderful manner conscience reveals that law which is fulfilled by love of God and neighbor. In fidelity to conscience, Christians are joined with the rest of men in the search for truth and for the genuine solution to the numerous problems which arise in the life of individuals and from social relationships."

This last expression is especially important, for we are not mature if we think that we need no longer search because we already know the truth while others do not. With the rest of men we are enjoined ever to deepen our knowledge of truth and to seek ways to apply it to individual and social problems of our times. Only the immature are content with ready-made answers to questions which leave them incapable of relating to people of different opinions and backgrounds.

The more a correct conscience rules, the more persons and groups will be encouraged to turn from blind choice and "be guided by objective norms of morality." The moralizer equates his own imperfect formulations with objective truth. He clings to static principles expressed in immobile language in order to avoid the risk of a personal decision. He accuses of restlessness and recklessness those who are protesting against lifeless customs and laws. However, only those who are constantly searching and striving in communion with others will attain greater maturity.

Vatican II frankly acknowledges that "conscience frequently errs from invincible ignorance without losing its dignity." These are strong words: although a Christian gratefully appreciates the guidance he receives through God's revelation and through the community of the faithful, he frequently errs through invincible ignorance; yet this can happen without personal guilt. As long as one sincerely seeks truth, his conscience maintains its dignity. "The same cannot be said, of course, of a person who cares little for the search for truth and goodness, or whose conscience has gradually grown sightless as a result of habitual infidelity."

"Invincible ignorance" is not at all stubborn self-sufficiency or complacency; it is the limitation of a person who is sincerely working toward a more perfect life. In his *Apologia Pro Vita Sua,* Cardinal Newman says, "I have always contended that obedience even to an erring conscience was the way to gain light."[2]

We understand conscience, then, as man's innermost yearning toward "wholeness" which manifests itself in openness to neighbor and community in a common searching for goodness and truth. Man's conscience is unthinkable without an active sharing of experience and insights with others searching for truth in mutual responsibility.

[2] New York: Modern Library, 1950; part VI, p. 212.

A Synthesis of Experience and Knowledge

(6) The more effectively one arrives at a *synthesis of all the experience and knowledge* he has acquired, the more he approaches wholeness as a person. Religious formation is not a collection of concepts, laws and devotions; it is the fundamental unifying force of an illumined faith that welds together all factors making for man's wholeness. It integrates his outlook by bringing into complete harmony his knowledge, will and action; it completes him.

Theology has a special mission for this unifying action, but it must not act as a tyrant, imposing its methods on other sciences. In the medieval world, when theology was the "queen of the sciences," theologians assumed they were competent to dictate methods and results to other sciences without self-examination, without acknowledging their own need to be enriched, corrected and possibly confronted by other insights.

Today it is evident that theology is not tyrannically imposing its methods. As a sacred science, a sacred and existential one, theology has its own specific methods. It is sacred to the extent that it opens our minds to God's light, integrates man's outlook and presents Christ's message of love in all personal relations, in all human potential and in all things.

Rightly understood, religion can uniquely contribute to a global view of culture, behavioral sciences and human problems leading to a holistic understanding of man and the universe. But here theologians must be cautioned against eliminating what they cannot fit into their narrow system. They must approach the wholeness of man and his relation to God from different angles, humbly admitting that some points do not fit into their system because of imperfections inherent in all human systems. Our integral function rests on our acknowledgment that God is infinitely greater than our knowledge and our finite outlook.

In our present culture, too many young people leave college with fragmented knowledge that lacks unifying perspectives because it is unrelated to such a central theme as the wholeness of man. If theology becomes a totally separated, watertight compartment, if it presents sterile dogmas unrelated to life, interprets morality as "do" or "don't" imperatives, Scripture as a separate entity, and dogmatic theology as unrelated to the biblical sciences; if it allows canon law to remain out of touch with the Bible and with modern society, one cannot expect this kind of theology to produce ministers of wholeness and salvation. How could such a theologian possibly help another man to become an integrated person? It is vital, therefore, that all religious formation, all theology focus on man's wholeness, seeking a vital synthesis. It is one of the theologian's most noble tasks to be a servant in our own culture, to help forward this process of integration.

The Continuity of Life

(7) A mature person *respects the continuity of life,* gratefully accepting the heritage of the past while being open to growth, development and beneficial change. There are

people who boast "I always have said this" or "I have always done that" and never intend to change. Some go so far as to say: "I cannot change; in allegiance to God, I have to remain what I am." This cannot be fidelity to the living God. The immobility of a stone is not a quality of the Christian character.

In the light of traditions, of history and of the present moment, the mature Christian judges all opportunities and expectations in view of the future. It is a decision that involves both a risk-taking courage and an expression of fidelity to the Lord of history. This type of person inspires and deserves trust. He is reliable, steady and faithful, but his fidelity is to God's design as it unfolds in the signs of the times, not in his own habits or opinions. Thus he stands ready to make changes in response to God's fidelity and in the light of the exigencies of an ever changing world and the new needs of man.

Principles vs. Rigidity

(8) A person of character has *principles;* yet, if he is mature, he never treats principles as rigid issues, never misuses them to justify automatic, impersonal and even heartless behavior. He probes for the values expressed by the principles and is guided by them. There have been sad examples of reasoning done in the name of principles. For instance, when the first experiments with the transplantation of organs were made, some famous moralists immediately stated that this was against the principle proscribing self-

mutilation. Just what does it mean to mutilate one's self? What is the meaning of life? Of integrity? What is the meaning of the whole person with all his personal involvements and relationships?

These moralists adjudged mutilation not in the total context of living but only in the partial act of removal of an organ. In their eyes, a mother who sacrificed an organ to save the life of her son or daughter while still being able to live fully as a person without it, violated the principle which does not allow mutilation of one's self. For their "objective morality," it made no essential difference whether the organ was thrown on the dunghill or given to save the child's life. Here, in a human sense, we have a wholly artificial solution to a vital problem, with no meaning, no integrative value-perspective.

The same erroneous fixation on humanly meaningless factors has been shown in similar matters such as birth regulation where the life situation dictates gaining insight into what the principles really stand for and what values they are supposed to protect. There are too many cases of "principles" being invoked and managed in a way so as to rationalize preconceived or stereotyped conclusions, or, at least, to evade the effort at deeper examination of the problem.

Genuine fidelity to principles goes hand in hand with fidelity to the living God, the God of history who incessantly manifests new facets of his design. Therefore, besides firm adherence to the values expressed in principles, faithfulness includes a constant effort toward a better expression and understanding of those values. Principles are not quotations from a dead language; they are communicators of deep insights in view of present opportunities.

The Need of Balance

(9) Many people focus only on abstract principles, laws and obedience. Others choose to concentrate only on freedom, initiative and spontaneity. Each party resolves the complexity in favor of his own bias. A mature Christian strives for a happy balance between the two.

Bare confrontation with abstract laws and principles, especially with man-made precepts supported by insistence on obedience and power, can only produce immature people. Today, it is likely to provoke rebellion or protest from more mature people, leaving only the less mature to conform to this pattern. On the other hand, arbitrariness likewise develops immaturity. Violent protest can also be a by-product of an arbitrary or formalized use of authority and "principles."

From above and below, authority and obedience must be seen in their proper relationship to love and justice. Do they contribute to the building up in love of a genuine community, a structured community? Only persons who live in the all-embracing perspective of love can build mature relationships in the realm of obedience and authority, with laws and structures that harmonize responsible obedience with genuine initiative. Achievement of this harmony is one of the great challenges of our times.

Self-Control and Effectiveness

(10) A person striving for maturity develops *self-control* to temper a rich affectivity. It was a most unfortunate error of some older ascetical writers to suggest that the mature person could exist without a highly developed affectivity, without passions. Many of the biographers of saints have pictured them without emotions, passionless, with no expression of joy, sorrow or wrath, never enjoying a friendship nor reacting in a human way. Whatever could not be accommodated into the biographers' way of thinking was omitted, for it would have been shameful for their saints to have done something human involving spontaneous passions.

Of course, passions can manifest or cause disorders. Passions without wisdom and control, without the direction of genuine, self-forgetting love, are simply dissipation. But there is no real force of faith, hope and love without passion. One need only look to the Beatitudes; all the passions, most of the emotions are represented: sorrow, joy, love of Christ, jubilation and staunch opposition to evil. A mature person does not stifle his passions; he directs his emotional energies with the firmness of love toward a clear goal.

Openness to Beauty

(11) *Openness to beauty* is another of the most essential aspects of Christian morality and maturity. In the Bible, the

key concept of the *glory* of God as well as of *grace* (graciousness) contains the aspect of beauty and attraction. God makes visible the splendor of his love. Most of the Psalms express admiration and jubilation over the beauty of creation, and the hymns of vespers give expression to admiration and joy because of the beauty of God's work in the history of salvation. In reading the Bible, one becomes aware of how God gave his gracious gifts to the craftsman, to the artist. And what importance religious art assumes when it captures the fire of life!

Appreciation of beauty and of creativity helps to liberate humanity from the impoverished view of stark utility and depersonalizing management. Even in religion, an all too pragmatic culture and an imperative moral theology produce a milieu that impedes personal growth toward maturity. If the whole value of beauty is suppressed, there is nothing left but the imperative approach: "Thou shalt, thou shalt not," or the commercial approach: "What will be the reward for good behavior?" The whole value of biblical reward then disintegrates, for the biblical reward is "glory," a splendor of graciousness, love, joy and beauty, of man's self-fulfillment through openness to God and to his work within him, sharing everything graciously with all.

A mature person admires God in his universe; he is astonished at the mystery of man. Admiration is one of the conditions of prayer, and if one wishes to be capable of religion and of prayer, one must learn to be sensitive to beauty.

In the spontaneous prayer of Teilhard de Chardin, we feel

the intensity of his love and admiration of God as he "sings" to him through the universe:

> Glorious Lord Christ: the divine influence secretly diffused and active in the depths of matter, and the dazzling centre where all the innumerable fibres of the manifold meet; power as implacable as the world and as warm as life; you whose forehead is of the whiteness of snow, whose eyes are of fire, and whose feet are brighter than molten gold; you whose hands imprison the stars; you who are the first and the last, the living and the dead and the risen again; you who gather into your exuberant unity every beauty, every affinity, every energy, every mode of existence; it is you to whom my being cried out with a desire as vast as the universe, "In truth you are my Lord and my God."

"Beauty," says Thomas Aquinas, "is one of the names of God." As such, it offers a limitless field for meditation because of God's bountiful gifts and the manifestations of beauty around us. Openness to beauty can exert a great power to liberate man from attitudes of violence and of abuse of people.

Humility and a Sense of Humor

(12) A truly mature Christian is *humble,* never thinking that he has achieved holiness but realizing that he is en route, always undergoing a continuous conversion.

The model for conscience formation that is given to us in

the Sermon on the Mount is one for a formation in growth. Its direction is the great affirmative, "Love one another as I have loved you. . . . Be all goodness just as your heavenly Father is all good." This directive orients us toward ever greater heights, to a constant searching for the next step in the order of love.

There is no room here for any one-sided attention to obligatory limits: "What is the minimum allowed?" or for the complacent "All this I have done since my youth," which is so often the effect of minimalism as proposed in an imperative system of laws and precepts. The self-satisfied person is the embodiment of immaturity. His self-sufficiency has dulled the fervor of love and he will never attain maturity.

A person striving for maturity recognizes his shortcomings, humbly acknowledges them, and may even exhibit a sense of humor in relation to them. It is a real breakthrough to be able, finally, to accept the burdens that have come to us through our heritage, through the psychological results of our environment and through our own limitations. We then begin to give them a new direction because we have enriched our perspective. For instance, we can finally love imperfect persons, both our neighbor and ourselves, with an understanding, accepting love that sees and reveres God in all his works.

Finally, I would say that it is in Christian humor that maturity is especially found. A mature Christian takes God and his work with the utmost seriousness and respects himself in view of God's love and patience, but he never takes himself too seriously. We all have temperamental quirks and indulge in idiosyncratic behavior, so why should we take ourselves too seriously? We need a sense of humor. Humorless people are almost always hopelessly condemned to immaturity. Or should we say that immature people are condemned to a humorless existence?

Protest and confrontation so often degenerate into violence today because of the lack of a sense of humor on one side or on both sides.

V

The Role of Conscience

If we casually ask people around us what they mean by the word "conscience," we are apt to receive a variety of rather inconsistent answers. The range becomes even wider if the people belong to different cultural or religious backgrounds. I shall attempt to present here a kind of typology of the various meanings of the word "conscience" in today's world, and then contrast this with some thoughts from the Bible and Christian tradition, though not necessarily in the exact context of conscience.

Constructive and nonviolent forms of protest, as well as the concepts of obedience and authority properly understood, all presuppose the existence and validity of the idea of conscience.

What Conscience Means to Contemporary Man

Modern man appeals to the concept of conscience when he protests against intolerance, prejudice, heartless legalism, blind obedience, and the ruthless violation of laws promulgated for the common good, especially those intended to protect the fundamental rights of man. People belonging to the free world protest against brainwashing because it is a method calculated to destroy the conscience of the individual.

Another common idea about conscience is that it has to do with responsibility. A man is considered to be "conscientious" if he has developed a sense of responsibility toward his neighbor or family, in professional or social relations, or in the area of civic obligations. This concept of a responsible conscience means that he has a vital awareness of the current needs of his fellowmen or the community. A man is said to have a "lively conscience" if he readily responds to the opportunities and responsibilities of his age and milieu.

The word conscience is sometimes used with regard to decision-making. A person may be said to have a "bad conscience" if he makes a decision that fails to correspond to the dictates of his conscience or has betrayed a lamentable lack of awareness. In such cases the chief interest is whether he has made a right decision. Modern man, by nature more inclined to look forward than backward, is not apt to spend much time on passive remorse for what he may have done in bad conscience, but he does review past decisions seriously with a view toward shaping the future. When troubled by undigested failures, he confesses to the psychoanalyst. He is anxious to learn from past failures how to make better decisions now and in the future.

While some moralists display an almost exclusive concern with conscience as decision-making, others envision the concept more as an ongoing, sincere intention to act according to one's own convictions internalized through sensitization to definite values. A man of conscience in professional life is worthy of trust. He has ethical standards; he knows what he is expected to do and acts accordingly. To him, conscience is primarily an attitude of honesty about values that are especially prized, honesty in the search for truth, honesty in the sincere expression of truth and in its practical application in business matters.

Discussions centering on conscience often arise when religious liberty and tolerance are being considered in our pluralistic society. The elite stratum of almost all social classes feel that faith, belonging to a church or similar organization, and even the acceptance of certain doctrines, must be a matter of personal conviction. A man is said to be a person of conscience if, in religious matters, he is strikingly earnest and sincere, more concerned with the search for truth than with conformity to the pattern of the social or religious group to which he belongs. In a pluralistic society, a person is judged not so much by membership in a certain religious group as by the extent to which this membership reflects the free decision of his own conscience. If it is a question of conviction, modern man has respect for a person belonging to a different religion. Tolerance as a moral attitude is based on respect for the conscience of one's neighbor, and unless there is strong evidence to the contrary, modern man does not doubt the sincerity of another man's differing convictions.

In discussions about conscience, a common pattern within a whole group may sometimes be challenged. What is done in the name of a group, without individual qualms of conscience, against the victims of group discrimination or against social justice or peace on earth, is often rationalized as being motivated by prejudice and therefore obviously not a valid form of true conscience.

In the past, a man could acquire quite a reputation for having an excellent conscience if he revealed that he was anxious and meticulous about legal minutiae. The word conscience would not even be mentioned in such a case today; at best, he might be said to have a "deformed conscience."

Formerly people were also said to have good consciences when they unfalteringly obeyed human laws and precepts. The obedient person was looked upon as having an integrated, upright, strict and safe conscience. Today, however, the word conscience is more frequently used with reference to those who act out of personal conviction, who actively oppose unreasonable or unjust laws or patterns of behavior, especially when no other attitude seems responsible.

Today's secular man frequently speaks about conscience in a way that suggests something akin to the Christian idea of salvation. For example, he speaks about the integrity of man's conscience. By preserving and developing the integrity and sensitivity of the conscience, he feels that he is preserving and defending the integrity of man as such.

I do not intend to discuss here all the pseudoscientific theories of those who confine their attention to some striking examples of superficial social conformity in order to prove that conscience is "nothing else but" a social game. Neither do I intend to deal with a Marxist theory of conscience that splendidly ignores all phenomena that do not fit into the theory that morality and conscience are "nothing else but" a superstructure in a dialectical process relating to economic life or a tool used in the power struggles between groups or churches. We are concerned only with those modern men who take conscience and morality seriously—although in differing senses—and therefore are ready to distinguish between a pseudo-conscience and the conscience of men who are earnestly seeking the good.

What Revelation Says about Conscience

A study of the meaning of conscience in the Bible could well begin with consideration of the word that most closely corresponds to our word "conscience," namely *syneidesis*. We would then have to investigate how the term is understood in Greek and particularly by Greek writers on ethics, and how the biblical authors borrowed and then transformed the term in their writings and theology. Then we would have to examine other words and phrases used by the biblical authors having meanings similar to that of *syneidesis*. But a complete study of what the Bible has to say about the idea evoked by this word and its peripheral connotations would have to go beyond mere questions of vocabulary. The Bible sometimes has very explicit and profound things to say about the concept of conscience when these words or phrases are not even used.

My purpose, therefore, is not to seek a bridge between the Greek use of *syneidesis* and its equivalents and biblical usage. As a moral theologian I see my task rather as a search for the bridge between the understanding of conscience by modern man and the light shed on this modern concept of the term by Revelation. It is most important, therefore, to see first how the biblical authors or the apostles and the early Christian community, or the Old Testament prophets, related the message of salvation to the various intellectual and cultural patterns of their day. Our task begins where the biblical philologist might consider his work as done.

Alertness as a Sign of Conscience

To the extent that the modern understanding of the phenomenon of conscience emphasizes the importance of vigilance, alertness, openness to present opportunities, it serves as a bridge to biblical thinking. The great prophetic theme of the Bible, reaching its climax in Christ, is meant to shock the formalist and legalist who is congenitally insensitive to the here-and-now needs of his neighbor or to the here-and-now dangers to man's integrity and freedom. The prophets are of course not enemies of worship, but they are intent on unmasking a soulless kind of worship, a ritualism that allows people to escape from any serious moral commitment to their fellowmen. In the gospel of the merciful Samaritan, the priest or Levite is the prototype of a man with a pseudo-conscience. He is a man dominated by routine, a careful observer of an intricate code of proscriptions. The Samaritan who saw the man fallen among robbers and left half dead is just the opposite; he is the prototype of the man who has a sensitive conscience and acts accordingly. "He saw him and had compassion" (Luke 10:33).

Christ himself is the man who waits for the hour which the Father has prepared for him. He senses the needs of those around him. From his church and all the People of God, he expects the constant vigilance of the virgins who remain alert for the coming of the bridegroom. "Awake sleeper. . . . Look carefully then how to walk, not as unwise but as wise: Use to the fullest the present opportunities" (Eph. 5:14–16). This is a central imperative weighing on the Christian conscience. Alertness, in the biblical sense, is in the final analysis confrontation with God or Christ. God calls. He prepares through his gifts this present opportunity. The person whose conscience is sensitive to this situation realizes that he cannot be truly himself, cannot reach salvation unless he is vigilant, grateful and outgoing. On occasion he will protest against structures and methods of exercising authority which betray a lack of this vigilance.

Since conscience is alerted by the coming and dynamic presence of God, Creator and Saviour, it pays attention not only to earthly needs and tasks but above all to the salvation of our human neighbor. The apostle Paul shows us how to renounce rights and privileges, how to adjust to the way of life that opens a door to the Gospel. His casuistry and his own example are an appeal to be alert to the needs of salvation, to the purity of the faith and hopes of weak fellow Christians. Faith and hope, if genuine, make the faithful alert to the *kairos* and urge them to do good to everybody, according to the gifts God has granted and the needs of neighbor as they reveal themselves.

The modern concept of conscience, when it emphasizes awareness of the real needs of neighbor and society, does not always do justice to the religious background; it often totally ignores it. God, salvation in God, is not even thought of when people speak about a sensitive and alert conscience. From a religious point of view, therefore, is this kind of conscience completely without value? Certainly not. It is seldom due to a desire to dismiss or ignore God but is simply the result of a lack of awareness of the religious foundations. If there is truly an openness toward others, it may merit the response of the Lord: "Truly, I say to you, as you did it to one of the least of my brethren, you did it for me" (Matt. 25:40). An alert social conscience about those who may be deprived or rejected, about colored people in the U.S.A. and the emerging nations where no gain for ourselves can be hoped for, all this is praised in the Bible. It deserves the name of conscience.

The Dynamism of Conscience

Conscience is not a kind of superstructure of the personality; it is the person in his essential dynamism toward wholeness.

Modern man, confronted with colleagues who know what to do but feel no strong impulse to act accordingly, would accuse such men of having weak consciences or even of being without conscience. Psychology shows how people go to pieces who constantly neglect to act according to their moral insights. If a person is to possess true inner unity, harmony, integrity and soundness, his mind must be open to true values and devoted to them; the will must be open to the known good and must be dedicated to it.

Conscience thus appears, in many respects, as a secular expression for salvation. Salvation is man in his total openness to God's saving love, an openness that bears fruit in charity, peace, joy. . . . Salvation comes dynamically from God. God's Revelation is an outpouring of holy fear and joy in which a man feels that his wholeness, his salvation, depend totally upon his acceptance of Revelation. This acceptance means the bringing forth of fruit in charity for the benefit of everybody.

In his deepest self, the human person is attracted by the living source of all truth and all goodness. He senses in the depths of his being how his own integrity derives from his response to the manifest goodness and holiness of God. In faithfulness and openness of conscience, there is a sign of God's dynamic presence. In refusal to act upon the "word" received by the human person, judgment is already in process. Man destroys himself gradually. He separates himself from God, the source of salvation.

The modern concept of conscience is reflected—though in a secularized sense— in the Sermon on the Mount: "What then of the man who hears these words of mine and acts upon them? He is like a man who had the sense to build his house on rock" (Matt. 7:24-27). The secularized man readily understands that faith without works means judgment, but he does not so readily realize that the just man lives by his faith. He does not see that faith vivifies man's conscience, brings him to integration and salvation. He still sees in conscience a dynamic reality but does not always recognize that its dynamism is given and sustained by the word of God, the Creator and Redeemer, and by the energy of faith which is a gift of God.

As long as modern man does not concentrate wholly on his own inner integration and fulfillment, as long as conscience means for him an openness to the Thou, to values, to persons, and to those who cannot repay him, we have here a fundamental structure that is still related to the structure of faith. There is a sign of God's hidden but real presence.

The Autonomy or Theonomy of Conscience

Men of the secular world no longer talk about faith and a life according to faith but about conscience and responsibility. In the biblical world there was less introspection; theological ideas were not expressed so often in psychological terms as in modern times. Primitive people do talk about the subjective dispositions of a conscience but speak about the voice that is calling them, about God within them, God who exhorts and quickens them. Man's innermost being is seen in terms of a free dependence on God and on the manifestation of his saving will. Man loses salvation and moral integrity as soon as he concentrates on his own ego without listening to God who is calling him. Eve and Adam, listening to the strange voice of the serpent, are involved in a monologue; they pay no attention to God, and thus deprive themselves of God's friendship. We might say they experienced the hazards of an autonomous conscience, one totally concentrated on the self. They have closed their ears to the voice of God as Father and Friend. But in spite of their hiding or flight from God, they cannot escape his reality and their dependence. Cain says: "From thy face I shall be hidden; and I shall be fugitive and a wanderer on earth. . . . Then Cain went away from the presence of the Lord . . ." (Gen. 4:14–16).

St. Paul reiterates the same theme in the Epistle to the Romans. Man's integrity—we would say man's conscience—depends on his openness to God. "Although they knew God they did not honor him as God or give thanks to him; therefore, they became futile in their thinking and their senseless minds were darkened. Claiming to be wise, they became fools. . . . Therefore God gave them up to the lusts of their hearts. . . . Since they did not see fit to acknowledge God, God gave them up to a base mind and to improper conduct" (Rom. 1:21–32).

Faith in the living God keeps man's heart and mind open, floods his innermost being with its light. Man must make his decision in the sight of God. Since God is Father and Redeemer of all, this decision must be made with keen sensitivity to the situation of one's neighbor. "If you have a clear conviction, apply it to yourself in the sight of God. Happy is the man who can make his decision with a clear conscience. . . . Anything that does not arise from conviction[faith] is sin" (Rom. 14:22–23).

The Bible shows that man's capacity to grasp the good is alerted by the grace of God, by faith, the gift of the Holy Spirit. One who entrusts himself to God in faith receives assurance in his conscience about decisive matters. On the fundamental question of the relationship of the Christian community to the Jewish people, Paul said: "My own conscience, enlightened by the Holy Spirit, assures me. . . ." (Rom. 1:9).

When modern man equates conscientiousness with personal responsibility, he reveals a heritage of biblical thought, though secularized. Faith is an existential response to God. The concept of responsibility includes the fact of "response." Is it response to a person, to another person, or chiefly to one's own need for integrity? Is it a response in view of things, rights, possessions? Insofar as modern man is sensitive to interpersonal relationships, to responsibility for the fundamental rights of all persons, there is a bridge to the biblical concept of faith-conscience. But where everything centers on self-conservation, independently of God, and where the "other" is seen merely as an occasion or condition for the development of one's self, there is that autonomous conscience that the Bible warns against and says is doomed to self-destruction.

Today's man must be asked explicitly what he means by

responsibility. Is it a total readiness to listen and respond to the One who has called us to togetherness in mutual responsibility? Does he search with all earnestness to understand the call to responsibility as coming not only from one's self and not only from abstract principles and values? Does the modern understanding of "conscience and responsibility" include, at least by implication, the responsorial understanding that in the Bible is expressed by faith?

Belief and Personal Conviction

Whereas modern thought centers on conscience and personal conviction, biblical thinking is expressed more in terms of faith: God speaks to man and man hears or refuses to hear. The emphasis is on the One who speaks; attention is given to the voice that is heard rather than to man's organ of hearing. Nevertheless, biblical thought takes man seriously. His thoughts, desires and deeds reveal his "heart," his innermost being, or else betray his self-centeredness and deafness. Revelation challenges the thoughts of man, even his religious beliefs. The unbeliever is questioned as to the righteousness of his heart. Has not the light in him become darkness? The world around the People of God is naïve and uncritical toward their religious thoughts and beliefs; Revelation awakens them to self-examination.

We have an analogous situation today. People often speak emphatically about the conviction of conscience, or simply about conscience, when they have made no effort to distinguish between genuine personal conviction and social and racial prejudices. It is true that modern man seldom asserts that he has heard God's voice and is acting out of faith; in fact, he is generally very critical of people or groups who make of their religious faith and conscience a self-serving business. (South African Calvinists who assert their superiority and defend their unjust privileges in the name of religious revelation are the exception in today's world.) But there is not yet the same critical sense toward the self and the group when people claim to have a conviction of conscience.

All this means a challenge for the believer to be especially careful when claiming to have personal conviction as matters of faith. Is he really sure that God spoke in this way? Has he a divine guarantee that his opinions and convictions are right? The believer must learn to distinguish between matters of faith and mere human convictions or even tentative opinions. Only in this way can believers challenge unbelievers who, in the name of conscience and conviction, refuse to accept the message of faith. Purity of conscience forbids confusion between prejudices and loyalty to one's own conviction, and the certainty of faith.

Faith, Freedom of Conscience, Tolerance

Faith is a free and joyous acceptance of Revelation, which is an unmerited gift of God. It does not tolerate coercion. One who trusts in the power of the Good News and the witness of genuine faith will never try to impose religious belief by force or earthly sanctions. The uniqueness of faith and the doctrine of grace must lead all believers to religious freedom.

However, religious tolerance, in a sense faithful to the Bible, cannot be understood as the mere absence of unjustified force. Rather, it is the firm conviction that nothing less than absolute brotherliness is necessary for the full witness of faith and conscience. If, therefore, men of good will are not yet convinced of the truth of Revelation, the Christian is not only forbidden to judge the conscience of the individual person who is a so-called "unbeliever"; he is further obliged to begin with judgment of himself. For the People of God must know that judgment begins with the house of God. Thus respect for the conscience of those who differ essentially from us in religious belief is intimately related to a humble examination of our own conscience.

With regard to this judgment that begins with the house of God, the *Pastoral Constitution on the Church in the Modern World* says:

> The believers themselves frequently bear some responsibility for this situation [of unbelief]. For, taken as a whole, atheism is not a spontaneous development but stems from a variety of causes, including a critical reaction against religious beliefs, and in some places against the Christian religion in particular. Hence believers can have more than a little to do with the birth of atheism. To the extent that they neglect their own training in faith, or teach erroneous doctrine, or are deficient in their religious, moral, or social life, they must be said to conceal rather than reveal the authentic face of God and religion. (Art. 20.)

The remedy which must be applied to atheism is to be sought in a proper presentation of the Church's teaching as well as in the integral life of the Church, led by the Holy Spirit who renews and purifies her ceaselessly to make God the Father and His Incarnate Son present and in a sense visible. This result is achieved chiefly by the witness of a living and mature faith, trained to see difficulties clearly and to master them. . . . What does the most to reveal God's presence, however, is the brotherly love of the faithful who are united in spirit as they work together for the faith of the gospel and prove themselves a sign of unity. (Art. 21.)

If this way of thinking and acting were followed by believers in all churches and religions, then the secular man would be given the necessary challenge. He would more easily learn not to interpret all kinds of tolerance and intolerance as manifestations of authentic convictions. He would learn to distinguish tentative opinion or group prejudice from the phenomenon of a genuine conscience.

Law and Conscience

The Bible praises God for the revelation of his saving will and the manifestation of his law. There is a distinction, but no separation, between the saving will of God and the law of God. The law of God appeals to man's innermost being because it is a revelation of his will to build a covenant of love with a people who can recognize his holiness and mercy. In the Old and New Testament it is clear that the believer is not allowed to sever covenant from law, or to abide by an abstract law without looking to the living God. The law, severed from its source, is separated from the living God and is dead and death-bringing for man's conscience. The law, taken in its right context, helps man's conscience, gives light and direction, though it never dispenses him from alertness. Instead, it makes man alert to the actual needs of his fellowmen and helps him not to misinterpret a situation selfishly.

Today's secular man shares to a great extent the believer's fundamental concern not to sever law from person. He wants to see all human laws as expressions of the dignity of man and as a means for mankind's protection. He believes that all moral principles should be applications of the one great reality of love and justice. But does this man always realize that this concern for a truly personal and person-related conscience and conscientious attitude toward law and principle is ultimately based on faith in the living God? It is the great task of believers to convince him. The testimony of a well-oriented life is the most effective form of confrontation.

Conscience and Repentance

Biblical Revelation shows clearly that man's conscience cannot be whole and redeemed without forgiveness and reconciliation. Forgiveness includes repentance on the part of man. The call to conscience in the Bible is often, indeed essentially, a call to repentance, and is directed toward the group as well as the individual person.

Only humility can close the gaping wound to personality when man has not followed his conscience by searching for truth or by acting according to sincere conviction. The conscience of man, created according to the image and likeness of God, is constantly endangered by man's sinfulness and by darkness in the world around him. Man always gains light when he follows the conviction of his conscience, even though his judgment may be imperfect and sometimes even wrong. By acting in conformity with his upright conscience, he becomes more receptive to the light that comes from God and that is, to some extent, embodied in the divine milieu, in the church and in everything that is good and just in the world around him. But the dynamism of the conscience that strives for wholeness and harmony of conviction and action is endangered if man does not humbly recognize his own shortcomings, his own failures to respond to his genuine insights. Danger threatens for the conscience when a man, after acting contrary to his convictions, does not plainly acknowledge the fact in sorrow and purpose of amendment. The biblical message shows us that man, by himself, cannot restore the integrity of his heart; he is invited to pray: "Create a clean heart in me, O God" (Ps. 50:12). He is invited and urged also to offer reparation for his faults.

Does the modern meaning of conscience pay sufficient attention to this matter of humility, repentance and reparation? It is up to believers to communicate this message more convincingly to today's secular man. This does not seem to be possible unless a greater role is recognized for a prophetic protest within the church challenging those in authority whenever a serious examination of the need for and willingness to undertake reforms is called for. For we cannot expect modern secular man to accept the call to repentance and reform voiced by the church unless he sees this spirit embodied in the church herself.

VI

The Authority Crisis in Today's World

Painful and trying as it may be, a crisis is not necessarily a bad thing. On the contrary, it can be a great blessing if it leads to greater maturity, if it makes people more aware of the need for openness and a readiness to change. The word "crisis" in Greek connotes discernment, or an appeal for the sharpening of one's sense of discernment. An authority crisis is bad if it is caused by an inappropriate use of authority or by a lack of awareness, on the part of those exercising authority, that changes are called for with respect to what authority is and how it should be used.

Today's waves of protests directed against the universities, racial discrimination, war and compulsory military service, even the communist establishment, are not intended to demolish or destroy authority as such. These movements are all directed toward certain changes which, in the eyes of the protestors, are necessary for the common good and the proper exercise of authority.

The short ministry of Pope John XXIII and Vatican Council II were the occasion for the peaceful explosion of an awareness that an authority crisis exists in the church. This awakening to a crisis situation was accompanied by an unprecedented hope that it could be solved or overcome positively. Vatican II did not cause the crisis—if by crisis we mean a lack of adjustment—but it did give rise to a worldwide consciousness that there was such a crisis and sharpened people's critical attitude toward the church; it also established higher standards by which to judge the proper meaning and exercise of authority.

The exercise of authority as well as the concepts of obedience and disobedience must be judged on the basis of moral criteria. Christian protest should reflect a moral consciousness. However, protest and criticism today are too often content with a dangerous moralism. Both protestors and authorities tend to moralize, whereas only a cool understanding of the situation can help.

The Solidarity of the Church and the World

Liberals who think that the authority crisis is due entirely to ill will on the part of the forces of reaction and counter-revolution are as wrong as arch-conservatives who accuse progressives of destroying church authority by their criticism and/or disobedience. Not only do both sides display a very biased attitude toward obedience but they tend to moralize in a very simplistic way. There can be no doubt that the authority crisis in the world and that in the church are very closely interrelated. It would indicate a serious estrangement on the part of the Church of the Word Incarnate if the latter were not intimately involved in the birth pangs of a new era. The joys and sorrows, hopes and anguish, tensions and growth of humanity are part and parcel of the church, if she is to be really close to men and if she cares for those who are the most sensitive and most vulnerable.

(1) In our lifetime we have witnessed horrifying misuses and abuses of power and authority. Names like Hitler, Stalin, Mao Tse-tung and Mussolini; the recent forcible occupation of Czechoslovakia by neighboring communist powers; the atom bombs dropped on Nagasaki and Hiroshima —all these things have traumatized thousands and even millions of people who will not recover from such experiences within a single generation. For some time yet we shall have to bear in patience and prepare to live with a collective neurosis in order to regain a healthier outlook. For those interested in apologetics, it is worth mentioning that German Catholics resisted Hitler more consistently and effectively than those residing in the dechristianized or Protestant parts of the country, but there is no point in gloating over the fact. Protestants were also greatly shocked when they realized how the old virtue of civic obedience and the laws were being made to serve unworthy ends.

The soul-searching of Catholics is still going on; consider

only the explosive reaction around the world, particularly among Catholics, when news reached them about the Bishop Defregger case. It is perfectly true that Captain Defregger displayed more courage and sense of responsibility than most army officers in similar circumstances. He dared to object twice to the cruel order received from his commander; and even while being supervised by two emissaries from the commander, he dared to reduce the scope of the executions. It is a debatable question whether a flat refusal to have anything to do with such an order would have saved more lives or possibly resulted in an even greater disaster. However, the case has reminded everyone about the shocking fact that criminals like Hitler enjoyed the support and scandalous "obedience" of people who for generations had learned only to obey superiors uncritically without ever asking why. It would seem fairer not to accord too much publicity to the Defregger case after the lapse of twenty-five years, particularly since the man never tried to hide the facts and has suffered because he was involved in such a horrible incident. Defregger was accused in the press of "blind obedience," but this was not the case. Nevertheless, there has been shock that a man involved in such a terrible tragedy is now a bishop of the Catholic Church; it is all part of the collective trauma. Is it any wonder, then, that sensitive laymen and theologians react vehemently, even despairingly when after such dehumanizing experiences they hear a powerful Curial cardinal say: "The pope has to be obeyed even if he is wrong"?

Catholic countries have experienced milder dictatorships

than Germany, Russia or China. However, it cannot easily be forgotten that they produced and for a long time supported such men as Mussolini, Franco, Salazar and Charles de Gaulle. How could they reconcile this sociopolitical support with the Catholic concept of authority and obedience?

The Oedipus complex is an abnormal phenomenon arising out of unhealthy father-son relationships. Sigmund Freud found that many people who defended themselves against an intolerant, tyrant-like father were suffering from a pathological love for their mother. Recent studies in various parts of the world have shown that in a sound partnership marriage and family where the father shares his authority with the mother, personality disorders of the Oedipus type are rare. But the fact remains that a considerable segment of humanity has been deeply affected by the recent experiences with the terrible misuse of authority which has resulted in a correlative misguided kind of obedience. The imprudent use or misuse of church authority must be seen cast against this background of human experience. People expect authority and obedience in the church to be a sign of redemption, an instrument of peace and freedom, a guide toward a more mature understanding of authority and obedience in the secular world.

(2) The rapid transformation of modern culture is one of the principal causes of the tensions and the crisis of authority in the world: "Today, the human race is passing through a new stage of its history. Profound and rapid changes are spreading by degrees around the whole world. Triggered by the intelligence and creative energies of man, these changes

recoil upon him, upon his decisions and desires, both individual and collective, and upon his manner of thinking and acting with respect to things and to people. Hence, we can already speak of a true social and cultural transformation, one which has repercussions on man's religious life as well. As happens in any crisis of growth, this transformation has brought serious difficulties in its wake."[1] Vatican II takes for granted that we are faced with a "crisis of growth," out of which some difficulties will arise in the normal course of an era of rapid change, while others will stem from a lack of awareness and discernment as regards the new situation.

The old structures of economic, social, cultural and political life are now seen as inadequate. Unfortunately, people's frame of reference when attempting to probe the new problems also turns out to be outdated and defective. Mummified solutions to antiquated problems cannot resolve the new problems peculiar to an entirely different historical age.

People in key positions, even when they are men of goodwill, often lack the necessary preparation for the new kind of leadership demanded by the contemporary scene. There are inequities in the way leaders are chosen in the field of economics and in the cultural, political and religious fields as well. In the economic sphere, the dynamism of progress and growth quickly and effectively eliminates those who cling to outmoded patterns and are therefore unwilling to take the lead or incapable of it. Thus, dynamic and progressive people, mostly among the younger set, take over. Of

---

[1] *Constitution on the Church in the Modern World,* Art. 4.

course, their avidness for success does not always serve the cause of all who are involved.

Since economic "progress" today sets the tone for everything, lack of progress is felt all the more keenly when in the fields of culture, education, politics and religion we encounter veritable dynastic citadels that are more interested in retaining power than in being leaders called upon to serve in a new age. Church structures reflecting the long period of close alliance with reactionary political forces and partially fossilized in their attitude to other churches cannot produce good leaders. As a matter of fact, such inadequate structures can effectively block the selection of good leaders more effectively than trade-union structures and political pressure groups do that are more concerned with their own survival than with the well-being and future of man.

(3) Many churchmen of high rank, and civic leaders as well, are desirous of serving the community and society to the best of their ability, but they are so engrossed in their workaday world that they have little time to spare for becoming up-to-date in their particular field, and worse still, they may not even be aware of the need. They are the prestigious bureaucrats who dominated the static periods in history but who are now heavy burdens and the targets of violent protests in our dynamic age. This is particularly true of the world behind the Iron Curtain, where a once revolutionary movement has degenerated into a kind of typical establishment with its sterile doctrinairism. A partial opening to, and economic competition with, the western world only promotes dissatisfaction with their own unproductive

system and creates the desire to change it. People in the free world of course abhor the notion of any kind of frozen revolution—a revolution perverted into an establishment and given to the constant abuse of power and authority—and they become even more critical if attitudes and practices along these lines are observed in their own countries or in parts of the church.

(4) Advances in science, technology and economics have brought about a certain fragmentation of life. Modern society is riddled by internal contradictions and tensions. There is, however, a tremendous yearning for synthesis, for meaning to life, but on the other hand it becomes increasingly difficult nowadays to survey the whole process of social life and growth when the mass media encourage and facilitate the confrontation of so many different cultures and subcultures. If those in authority do not reveal a real ability to unify energies and guide humanity toward the fulfillment of its longings, they are distrusted and criticized. Recent outbursts of protest show that people are concerned because they do not want to lose their identity, their sense of purpose. How can those having authority in the family, society, state and church fulfill this unifying role if they have no intuition themselves of a synthesis of the total meaning of life?

The universities ought to have produced leaders capable of working out such a synthesis, but they failed in the crucial task, as have most of the seminaries and schools of theology, which should have turned out prophetic men for the church and society at large. Ethical prophetism is characterized by an appeal to wholeness and synthesis. Authorities who unduly insist on minutiae, who are interested only in displaying their power as regards dead or secondary issues while overlooking the possibility of synthesis, the wholeness of the human person and of the common good, are a real source of anxiety to persons alive to these vital issues. The situation naturally gives rise to genuine explosions of indignation and unrestrained violence.

(5) Contemporary man as a citizen of the church and the world is keenly sensitive to mankind's need for unity and solidarity. This yearning is generally shared by the authorities, but they often find themselves in a difficult situation with vested interests, traditions, career-mindedness and ideologies all forcing them to yield to pressure groups. Therefore, whatever effort is expended on the pursuit of unity, or lack of such effort, becomes damaging to their credibility with respect to this grave concern of humanity.

(6) The generation gap has never before been so sharply delineated as it is today, to the point where a ten-year span means greater changes within a generation and greater distance between generations than fifty or a hundred years in former eras. By themselves generation differences could be a source of mutual enrichment and creativity. When humanity fails to recognize the opportunity, as is the case today, it is chiefly due to a defensive attitude on the part of the older generation and specifically on the part of those in positions of authority. Youth become less docile as a reaction, and the vicious cycle goes on.

(7) An age marked by cross-cultural encounters, mass

media communications and manifold technological strides is bound to foster a more acute critical sense. The more vibrant and responsive segments of society realize today more than ever that they would be unable to resist the hidden seductions and persuasions or check the trends toward totalitarianism without a keen critical sense. Unfortunately, authorities often become angry or bewildered if the objects of critical scrutiny happen to be their own views and practices.

(8) That people in authority today are subjected to more vitriolic criticism than at other periods in history is no sign that their failures are greater or their shortcomings more obvious. It is simply that the standards expected of those in authority are higher than ever before; faults which at other times would have been condoned without difficulty are now condemned openly. The open criticism frequently expresses the hope that the situation can really be changed for the better, while lack of criticism is often expressive of a kind of despair and lethargy.

Particular Causes of the Authority Crisis in the Church

The situation in the church is very complex. In many respects, the church has taken into account the new style of life. Humility, selfless service and genuine readiness to accept criticism have considerably increased respect for church authority. However, the Second Vatican Council's efforts to bring about needed reforms have not been cordially received by certain prelates or tradition-minded laymen. Tensions have arisen and are likely to persist until there is a consensus about the underlying causes of the unrest.

(1) The Gospel, a revolutionary force of nonviolence, directs us to present opportunities. Often, however, we find that certain religious bodies have become very conservative, not to say regressive. No one questions the rightful concern of church authorities for the faithful stewardship of the legacy of truth entrusted to the church by Christ. It is also generally agreed that it would be imprudent to discard all past human experience and valid traditions. A number of factors, however, have contributed to placing religious leaders in the precarious situation in which they now find themselves, namely, that of being unable or lacking the willingness painstakingly to distinguish divinely revealed salvation-truth from human experience and formulas. Quite a few high-ranking traditionalists in the church seem unable to distinguish the divine message from human formulations which bear the mark of a certain cultural period in salvation history.

(2) The division of Christians into a number of separate churches contending with each other has resulted in a misplaced emphasis on secondary things: man-made laws and structures, and artificial distinctions. As the natural consequence of their defensive and polemical outlook, the various churches have not had the courage to examine closely what form of authority would best correspond to the Gospel while meeting the changing needs of men at different historical epochs.

(3) The sudden eruption of ecumenism has shaken the foundations of some segments of Christianity. Like a Pentecostal storm stirring the dry dust and dead bones, ecumenical enthusiasm has endangered some genuine values, especially where the spirit of prayer and contemplation was found wanting in needed vigor and depth. Most religious leaders are greatly concerned over church unification and sincerely talk about the longed-for unity of all Christian believers. However, seldom do church authorities realize all the implications of unity; they continue unnecessarily to emphasize points that are neither divine nor helpful to unity. Because of their earlier formation which cannot be totally overcome and/or due to the inertia generated by large bureaucracies, too many church leaders remain bound by formulations, traditions and structures that do not convey the message of the living God, the God of history and Lord Jesus Christ who came to remove barriers in order to gather all around Him. Perhaps it is too much to expect religious leaders and theologians in a few years to move away from the narrowness of centuries and to lower until they have successfully destroyed the artificial barriers erected in earlier days less sensitive to unity in variety and variety in unity.

(4) The biblical renewal coupled with a stronger historical-sociological consciousness on the part of today's Christians has created a gap and deepening conflict with more traditionally trained churchmen in positions of authority. While the former group is extremely alert to differences between the concept of authority as found in the Bible and that of the Constantinian era, many church leaders—though

good men essentially—remain totally unaware of such differences; as a consequence, they make the mistake of confusing divinely entrusted authority with the traditional image of church authority.

(5) The bare fact that history has recorded abuses of authority in the church or that the church has been excessively wedded to worldly power structures is not necessarily disturbing to sensitive, sensible and sincere persons. However, the persistence with which today's churchmen continue to employ a style of authority and language which disclaims past sins and mistakes on their part is what arouses bewilderment and anger and incites protest on the part of those who believe in the church and her mission. In this day and age, we remain incredible if we fail to assume the burden of history.

(6) In our mechanized and fragmented world, the community of faith is expected to provide help in integrating all aspects of life, in arriving at a synthesis of meaning. However, this synthesis can no longer come from the pope's exercise of power directly over the secular world, the temporal order, with theology being acclaimed as "the queen of all sciences" and imposing its methodology on all other disciplines. The church of Vatican II explicitly acknowledges the autonomy of the various sciences and of the temporal domain of life. The problem remains as to how the new synthesis will properly evaluate the relative autonomy of all the sciences in view of the all-embracing Kingdom of God and the universal mission of the church. For instance, the teaching office of the church has to take a stance on

natural-law ethics, on the meaning of human life in natural-law terms. But how can it fulfill its role in the modern world if it does not fully evaluate the new situations, ignoring somehow the broader shared experiences and co-reflection of mankind?

(7) Society-in-transition makes it difficult for the church or any other institution to present a unified image of itself. All the more is this true of the authority images reflected by our church leaders; some conflicting images can be traced to the insufficient preparation of our religious leaders or to their failure to keep abreast of sociological developments. The same men who are prophetic, clearsighted and forward-looking on certain issues can appear to be very static, even regressive, on others. This state of affairs can also be accounted for in part by the variety of viewpoints found in the immediate psychological environment of our church leaders and theologians. It is not an unusual occurrence for certain church leaders out of a primary concern for peace and unity within one's constituency to adopt a middle-of-the-road position between the opposing views of other administrators around them. But this middle-of-the-road position is the target of severe criticism on the part of many enlightened laymen and priests who see it as a step backward in the forward march of history. The middle position is not easily reconciled with the broader perspective of the unity of all of mankind or of those who look to the future.

(8) The long history of church-state relations, of the alliance between throne and altar, has without doubt been detrimental to the church. Even today, many church leaders

allied with the rich and powerful are more concerned with maintaining the status quo than with promoting religious belief. The Church of England has gradually come to realize that it is no advantage to religion to be a state church. The younger Catholic clergy and a considerable number of committed laymen in Italy and Spain are aware of the same thing. Yet church authorities today cling to the status quo, and all the more fanatically because of the rising protests of youth. Cardinal Suenens, in his now famous interview, rightly pointed out that the present system of papal diplomatic representation by archbishops (mostly Italians) presents the church in a false light and is a misrepresentation of what it is supposed to be. Is the church of the poor crying out for reform as well represented by these prelates as the church of the powerful rich who oppose reforms?

(9) The Gospel warns against ostentatious titles and career-seeking. I think that bishops and popes of the past erred when they aligned themselves so thoroughly with the feudalistic system, sharing the glory of princes, kings and emperors, living in lavish palaces, decked out in regal vestments and wearing the jewels befitting their titles. Why is the church today so unwilling to adjust to the modest style and titles of modern democratic leaders? Why all the insistence on outmoded vestments, titles and promotions? A College of Cardinals consisting of a self-perpetuating body comprising a sizable number of prelate-diplomats interested primarily in the career aspect of their work and with a high percentage over eighty does not seem to be the best way to guarantee a succession of worthy popes. Changes have been

made in the way bishops are chosen, but this is still a far cry from the simple method of choosing bishops in the primitive church, an age much less democratic than our own. Some recent appointments have led people to believe that those responsible for them were either totally unaware of the existing authority crisis, or were trying to instigate even wider protests.

(10) It seems that immobile, regressive church leaders enjoy a longer life span than dynamic leaders; they are also more averse to the idea of retirement. They have enjoyed for too long the frankincense rendition of "Thou art priest forever" and take it to mean eternal attachment to their dignified office rather than to Christ. It so happens that many of the older conservatives came from a patriarchal family background and remain alien to the partnership concept of family; yet it is a pattern which now applies to the use of authority in the church and in the secular world. For them, the church remains a monarchy with a centralistic constitution or a patriarchal family: if monarchical episcopacy was an adequate adjustment for the sake of greater relevance in an earlier age, it is truly not so today; it was never really consistent with the Gospel concept of authority.

(11) At a time when absolutism reigned supreme, the church was looked up to as an institution which successfully resisted the temptation to be despotic. Strangely enough, however, when the secular world moved toward a style of authority marked by subsidiarity and democracy, the Catholic Church and other religious bodies trailed behind or condemned new forms even for secular governments. In his

famous "Syllabus" of December 8, 1864, the last of the propositions condemned by Pius IX read: "The Roman Pontiff can and must be reconciled with progress, liberalism and modern culture." Without further distinctions, this proposition was included among "those wicked opinions and doctrines which the Pope condemned by the power of his Apostolic Authority" and all sons of the church were informed that they were to consider all these propositions "as rejected and thoroughly condemned."

The Catholic Church in recent centuries has an impressive record of opposing and condemning things which are later on regarded as praiseworthy and normal. On the other hand, the church has consistently counted in its ranks prophetic men, true pioneers of things to come. The church has produced great popes who can help us forget the condemnation of Copernicus, Galileo, Rosmini and other great thinkers, as well as the solemn approval of compulsory torture and the burning of witches. The greatest of these prophetic men in recent times has been Pope John XXIII, whose charismatic nature is acknowledged by men of all faiths. The fact that his most vehement critics were conservative Curialists and their friends introduced a new kind of protest because their venomous attacks and the ensuing protest were directed not only against the prophetic spirit but against the pope; therefore, it also meant a direct confrontation with the authority of the church. Those prelates who proclaimed that a hundred years would not suffice to correct the blunders and mistakes of Pope John lack credibility when they now pointedly censure dissidents who disagree with one point of a papal encyclical. Churchmen who opposed Vatican Council II claiming that "Nothing was taught with infallibility" only prove how inconsistent they are when they teach that popes have to be obeyed even if they are wrong. Extremism on the right, namely, on the part of powerful conservatives, is one of the reasons why we are now contending with extremism of the left.

Ways of Overcoming the Authority Crisis

Since the crisis of authority is neither a purely secular nor a purely religious phenomenon, we must search for solutions at all levels. The church has a significant role to play in arriving at solutions, because in the church the divine and the human meet in a most immediate manner. What can the church contribute to strengthen divinely willed authority in the social realm? How can she solve her own problems without forgetting, even for a moment, her service to the world and her being in the world? What are the common and respective roles of the church and society in sensing and utilizing the constructive elements of the contemporary situation? What will be the unique contributions of each?

(1) In the first place, I would like to mention the *prophetic role* in both the church and society. The prophets of the Old Testament made great demands, had courageous words of discernment and constructive criticism for the bearers of authority in church, state and society. Only when the official church and the People of God are willing to

receive and to act according to the prophetic appeal of genuine criticism can the church herself exercise her prophetic office with regard to the powers of this world. The church would do well to take seriously the world's criticism of her in the light of the divine admonition to constant renewal.

It would be a dangerous error for ecclesiastical office-holders, on the pretext that they are responsible to God alone, to stiffen their resistance to partially justified criticism instead of seeking a healthy dialogue from which both sides could learn. The kings and high priests of the old covenant were the "anointed of God"; yet God did not usually guide them by visions and dreams but often by very unpleasant admonitions and warnings on the part of daring men and women of prophetic character.

(2) I am convinced that we need more prophetic voices who will dare to speak out against superficial and destructive criticism, regardless of any popularity polls. However, it is clear that officeholders who come under the cross fire of criticism will hardly be heard if they try to defend themselves vehemently against their critics. At the present time, a change of roles might perhaps be desirable, with officeholders becoming above all prophetic voices leading us forward without removing themselves from challenging criticism, while theologians and publicists, who enjoy a certain prophetic role and the prospect of being heard, should at the right psychological moment speak out boldly on behalf of authority.

(3) The Catholic Church has only gradually liberated

herself from ideas of domination over worldly powers and alliances between throne and altar. Since she has begun this severance from earthly powers in a convincing manner, she has once again become a prophetic voice in the world. Suffice it to recall the great social encyclicals from Leo XIII to John XXIII and Paul VI. But only when the church has fully realized that the earlier adaptations are now obsolete and no longer make sense will she be able to make her full contribution to the resolution of the crisis of authority both within her own ranks and in secular society. It seems, for instance, that the system of diplomatic representation in the church needs further reform.

(4) In view of the general nature of our pluralistic and dynamic society, *deliberate training for genuine constructive criticism* seems to me an absolute prerequisite. In an epoch of mass-communications media and large-scale organization, man can retain the precious value of freedom only if he is "critical," that is, if he learns the art of discernment at all levels. If those who hold responsible positions refuse to recognize the positive value of criticism, those who possess dynamic energies will run wild in their criticism while those who are inclined to docility will obey not only legitimate but also illegitimate lords and commands. The true solution lies in giving criticism its rightful place in the roundelay of virtues, so that constructive criticism combined with self-criticism may be clearly distinguished from destructive and hostile criticism. This process of domesticating criticism may be compared to the transition from the hunters' culture to that of peasants and shepherds. Bearers of authority who

today reject all criticism or who go further and think that they must always be pursuing their critics return, so to speak, to the culture of the totem hunters.

(5) The transformation of wildfire criticism into the constructive criticism protective of freedom is possible only within the framework of an *ethic of responsibility* and within a form of society compatible with it, i.e., one which fosters the full participation of all in assuming responsibility in all the areas of life. The one-sided ethic of obedience thrived in the soil of a closed, static society. Today it must give place to a deep-rooted ethic of responsibility aimed at men who have come of age and are capable of discrimination for themselves. Naturally, the virtue of obedience has its rightful place alongside the virtues of humility and simplicity on the part of officeholders in a Christian ethic of responsibility and co-responsibility. The effort to make collegiality more effective is only one of the aspects of co-responsibility.

(6) The demand for the best possible *representation in the election or appointment of decisive bearers of authority* points in the same direction. It is evident that the mere right of succession or longevity of service does not qualify one for the exercise of authority. The common good demands the most competent person at a given time. Broad participation in the finding of appropriate persons for important functions and offices serves the purpose of the greatest *moral* prestige of the governing body far better than the secret consultation of a few who may be incompetent or may be moved by vested interests. A bold revision of the whole

system of electing and appointing ecclesiastical superiors can no longer be postponed if we are to be truly concerned about the moral prestige of these officeholders and want to meet the present crisis of authority effectively.

(7) All authority comes from God and there is no true authority which is not confirmed by God (Rom. 13:1). This passage is particularly applicable to ecclesiastical authority. Christ himself established the ministry of the apostles and the office of Peter as a service. Consequently, neither criticism nor new rules for the election and appointment of ecclesiastical officeholders should weaken the authority of pope, bishops or clergymen, much less destroy it. It behooves us all to contribute to a better understanding and more effective strengthening of genuine authority.

The positive purpose, however, is certainly not served by appealing too quickly to the divine origin of authority in cases where, in reality, the discussion concerns only the historically conditioned form of appointment, promotion or election. One can certainly say that, in the opinion of many, the question of the retirement age of bishops and priests has not yet been satisfactorily resolved. An eighty-year-old bishop who has lost contact with his people, particularly youth, and whose exercise of authority provokes either a public revolt or silent falling away from the church assuredly does not exemplify charity in service. When he further seeks to justify his refusal to make way for a more competent person by appealing to the divine institution of the episcopal office, he is only eroding genuine authority. We offend the authority of God himself when we seek to make him responsible for that which is all too human, whereas the solution can only be sought in humble conversion and reform.

Maximizing the Potential in the Present Crisis

There is no spiritual penicillin capable of checking the virulence of the authority crisis or the general crisis of growth both in the church and in the world. There can be no escapism to an "if and but" position. The appeal of the Lord of history is to "use to the best the present opportunities" (Eph. 5:16). Let us face reality with trust in God and a readiness to bear the burdens of each other, and the authority crisis will become for us a moment of God's favor. In a common effort, let us seek answers to: What are the best remedies? In a realistic way, how can we make best use of the present difficulties?

VII

Freedom and Authority in the Church

Johann Christoph Hampe, a Lutheran pastor and theologian, called the three large volumes on Vatican Council II which he edited, significantly, *The Authority of Freedom.* Karl Barth warmly praised this choice of title and the book's unique approach to the problems of the council. How much authority can freedom really be said to have in the Catholic Church since Vatican II? Does authority as exercised in the church really protect, safeguard and foster genuine freedom?

In a higher *complexio oppositorum* there is surely no opposition between freedom and authority. Ideally, the freedom of the children of God has authority and imposes its dignity on all, especially on those who are "in authority" and who consequently are servants of salvation, love, freedom and peace. But in daily reality the contrast-harmony is not so perfect. Not all people have the same understanding of authority or the same ideas about freedom.

Today we are faced with an urgent need to develop a theology of freedom. Man now has more liberty to shape his own "nature" and destiny than ever before. He has at his disposal various new forms of knowledge. Humanity is preparing not only to make more trips to the moon and to exploit the potentialities of atomic energy but it is also entering the age of genetic engineering. Man today has achieved an unprecedented mastery over matter and his ingenuity is expressed in countless inventions. It is within his power to shape biological and psychological tendencies by manipulating hereditary traits so as to produce new changes systematically.

In view of all this, is modern man sufficiently aware of the kind of freedom for which he should be ultimately striving? What kind of structures must there be to insure or to protect the proper use of freedom?

We have seen in our lifetime terrifying examples of tyranny, the treading underfoot of the most basic rights of human beings. Demagogues and advertisers with their thousand ways to influence people unconsciously are becoming ever more skillful in imposing decisions on us. It is only by means of the optimal development of modern man's own critical sense that he will be prepared to protect himself against the pressures and powers of a managed and exploited public opinion. If there is not a constant, communitarian concern with the proper use of freedom in the world around us, in our political and social institutions, our culture and customs, liberty as we know it cannot be expected to survive. If it wants to survive, it too must evolve in accordance with the new opportunities and needs.

To this threat the existentialist responds in his own special way. He feels that life will stifle his freedom if he does not direct his attention to the highest good of the person. But modern existentialism often fails to see that the freedom of persons can only be preserved if the persons themselves evince real concern for healthy structures and customs, and if the structures and institutions themselves are fully sensitized to the ideal of human freedom.

We need not only freedom as a great leitmotif but the elaboration of a theology of Christian freedom; we also need an active, concrete search for all the realistic ways in which freedom can be fostered and the right use made of it at this critical moment in salvation.

Reviewing the History of Salvation

St. Paul stresses the freedom of the Christian. Christianity must not become enslaved to human traditions. The Gospel must not be blocked by national narrowness. Freedom for Christ and for one's neighbor must not be hampered by legalism. Unselfish love in following Christ frees man from the slavery of sin and from the fear of death. Paul elaborates a theology of the freedom of the sons and daughters of God under the authority of the Gospel, in total dependence on God's liberating grace, in the fellowship of the Spirit and in a spirit of humble service. But did not Paul exercise his own authority in a somewhat paternalistic manner? Did he not confirm the patriarchal pattern of authority in marriage and the family? Only if we see his word and work in the perspective of history can we do justice to him. In his own time, Paul did the best he possibly could—not the abstract ideal—to promote greater freedom for women as well as for slaves. Later generations must not stop where he began.

A given style of authority—and I also include the style of church authority which is supposed to protect and foster freedom or limit it—is conditioned to a considerable extent by historical circumstances. It is therefore from limitations on freedom that had their origin in past history rather than from faith in Christ as such that the church must now liberate herself. Thus faith can be strengthened and purified.

During the earliest Christian centuries the basic patriarchalism of family life influenced the structure of the churches. They were built around a household or according to the image of a patriarchal household. The bishop exercised his authority more or less as the Roman paterfamilias did. The persecutions further tended to strengthen the authority of bishops. This authoritarian pattern consistent with the times also reflected the evangelical spirit of service, humility, solidarity and love. Paternalistic concern was as much appreciated then as it is disdained in our dynamic age when everybody strives to better himself and have a say in authority.

The age ushered in by Constantine and continued by

Charlemagne and Otto I brought about certain discordant changes in the concept of church authority. Bishops came to exercise more and more civil in addition to their ecclesiastical authority, or at least they adopted the style of the public officials of that period. The concrete style which became associated with the papacy was conditioned by the interaction of religious and social factors, the church-state controversy, the role of the pope as center of international political relations, and especially his role as a local Italian potentate. Feudalism, centralism and absolutism have all at various times influenced the church's structures and ideas about its own authority.

The basic German ethos was always absolute loyalty to the tribal leader or ruler. That is why the conversion of the German rulers was usually followed by the baptism of all their followers en masse. The scandalous principles of *Cuius regio eius et religio* in the sixteenth century showed all too clearly that this old idea of absolute loyalty to rulers was capable of being extended even to the sphere of individual religious convictions. The post-Reformation period saw the church in a posture of self-defense and resorting to some extent at least to types of control associated with closed societies.

Today the radical and rapid changes that are taking place in society and cultural relations are forcing the churches to adopt a new style of authority and to have a critical look at some of their inherited forms and concepts. It is not easy, however, to demythologize such a complex reality. We cannot simply return to biblical formulas, even though we must test everything by the spirit of the Gospel. Part of the *aggiornamento* of Vatican Council II is concerned with seeking a true synthesis between freedom and authority and expressing this in faithfulness to the spirit of Christ. This synthesis will be of great help if it can acclimatize itself in today's world and meet the needs of the present age.

Freedom and Pluralism

Vatican II brought about a thorough reexamination of what is meant by freedom of thought and expression in the light of a recognition of the need for greater pluralism in the church. It held that freedom could be accorded a greater scope without destroying the unity of the Catholic Church. Many topics which had previously been taboo were brought up for examination and frank discussion. It soon became obvious that the council had also achieved a kind of inner freedom to be able to listen to observers from the other churches and, finally, to listen to its own critics, including even atheists (e.g., see *The Constitution on the Church in the Modern World,* Art. 19–21).

An example of this frankness and freedom of expression was the speech delivered by the Melkite Patriarch Maximus IV at the council on the subject of birth control; he called for the setting up of a commission that would comprise not only Catholic laymen and theologians but men and women from other churches as well and even other religions. The papal commission on population problems first set up by

Pope John XXIII and later enlarged by Paul VI included only Catholics as members; nevertheless, the commission was constantly aware of what the modern world was saying on the subject through priests and laymen who were in touch with non-Catholics. Although Pope Paul did not approve the recommendations of the commission majority, one thing is certain: he encouraged the frankness of discussion and freedom of expression which all had wished for. In fact, by so doing he opened up an avenue to the future which cannot be closed again. When Cardinal Ottaviani was appointed chairman of the commission, he informed its members that he would normally not take part in the discussions or meetings because his chief task, as he conceived it, was to guarantee an absolute freedom of discussion and expression of thought, and some might feel that his presence would diminish rather than promote the desired freedom.

The council acknowledged that a far-reaching pluralism was an unavoidable consequence of the search for truth and the effort to find an adequate expression of it. Respect for truth itself obliges the church, in humility, not to offer solutions in only one sense when problems are of great complexity. Thus the council left open the solutions to many burning issues and warned, "Let the layman not imagine that his pastors are always such experts that, to every problem that arises, however complicated, they can readily give him a concrete solution, or even that such is their mission. . . . Often enough the Christian view of things will itself suggest some specific solution in certain circumstances. Yet it happens rather frequently, and legitimately so, that with equal sincerity some of the faithful disagree with others on a given matter."[1]

Vatican II declared that there cannot exist "a contradiction between those divine laws pertaining to the responsible transmission of life and those pertaining to the fostering of authentic conjugal love."[2] But in no way does it assert that it has the final answer on how to harmonize these two responsibilities, particularly in view of the population explosion and new insights into psychological factors. Instead, it appeals to everyone to learn the art of "distinguishing eternal realities from their changing expressions" and asks especially those "skilled in medical, biological, social and psychological sciences" to help find acceptable means of "proper birth regulation."[3]

A Theology of Evangelical Freedom

A sudden new impetus toward freedom and free speech would not of itself inspire great hope if it were not rooted in a deeper theological understanding. I do not maintain that the Second Vatican Council has produced a complete theology of the authority of freedom, but it has set the tone and pointed the way.

Among the important elements of a theology of freedom and of an authority that serves true freedom, I assign first

[1] *On the Church in the Modern World*, Art. 43.
[2] *Ibid.*, Art. 51.
[3] *Ibid.*, Art. 52.

place to a *renewed understanding of the mystery of the church*. An authoritarian style often equated "church" with "hierarchy," as if the pope and bishops were the church and the others were more or less outsiders or simply members subject to the "church." The original schema on the church prepared by theologians of the Holy Office stressed the hierarchical aspect; however, the council decided on a totally different approach.

The *Dogmatic Constitution on the Church* begins with the perspective of the Mystical Body of Christ and its many functions, the messianic People of God gathered around Christ and united by the gifts and charisms of the Holy Spirit. It is noteworthy that the chapter on the Messianic People of God (chapter II) begins with the prophecy of Jeremiah (chapter 31, verse 31), the law of God written in the heart and mind of his people. Neither Latin nor any man-made law nor any imposed uniformity can guarantee real unity; the *Holy Spirit* is the only guarantor of unity, a unity which includes *variety and diversity* as very valuable aspects. "In their variety all bear witness to the admirable unity of the Body of Christ. This very diversity of graces, ministries and works gathers the sons and daughters of God into one, because 'all these things are the work of one and the same Spirit'" (I Cor. 12:11).[4]

The constitution presents the laity not as "subject to authority" but rather in their own active responsibility. The chief role of the ministerial priesthood is to bring all to the

---

[4] *Dogmatic Constitution on the Church,* Art. 32.

fullest awareness of their belonging to the priestly People of God. The layman has not only a role in the church; he should also have a voice. "The laity should openly speak to pastors about their needs and desires, with that freedom and confidence which befits sons of God and brothers in Christ. An individual layman, by reason of the knowledge, competence or outstanding ability which he may enjoy, has the right and sometimes the obligation to express his opinion on things which concern the Church."[5]

A very important aspect of a theology of freedom in obedience to the Holy Spirit and in service to the community is the doctrine with respect to charisms. The authoritarian minority of the council fathers reacted sharply against the draft version of the constitution which stressed the importance of charisms and the spirit of spontaneity, creativity and initiative. Cardinal Ruffini was spokesman for some of them when he declared that while charisms were good and necessary in the time of the apostles, the church today should not expect to encounter them or have to speak so highly about them. He felt that to do so would undermine the power of those in authority and thereby threaten unity and order. The drafting commission reacted to this suggestion by strengthening the passages relating to charisms.

The Holy Spirit is the source of the freedom of the sons and daughters of God. The church can be a bulwark of freedom only to the extent that she is docile to the promptings of the Spirit in all her members. Hence, pastors should

[5] *Ibid.,* Art. 37.

not view their task as that of stifling the Spirit but rather they should discern the spirits. Above all, ministers and pastors of the church should not be administrators but truly charismatic men. Leadership in the church is meant to be leadership toward maturity for all.

Important, then, is the concept of *shared authority* or *collegiality* in the service of church governance. Pius XI, in his encyclical *Quadragesimo Anno*, declared that the principle of subsidiarity is the most fundamental principle of Catholic social doctrine. What can be done in free spontaneity in interpersonal relationships must not be taken over by the community. The special contribution of the community is to enable each person to fulfill his personal task. What the smaller community can accomplish well should be reserved to it. The larger community and the higher authorities should above all be concerned that the smaller community develop its own initiative and ability fully and responsibly.

The idea of subsidiarity does assign a rightful place to authority, but it is a "look from below," from the person to the more organized forms of community. Those in higher authority should not diminish the legitimate autonomy of individuals and smaller communities but rather strengthen it, although always in the direction of genuine solidarity. This spirit of solidarity fosters greater liberty and more effective subsidiarity, whereas a bare and uncooperative individualism simply provokes those in authority to attempt to check it through ever more authoritarian forms of law and control.

The principle laid down by Pius XI for modern society did not seem to be readily applicable to the structures of the church herself. Naturally, many asked: "Can the church apply this principle of subsidiarity to her own life?" Pius XII replied with a resounding "yes." The council took a necessary step in the direction of a theological and practical application with the idea of *collegiality*, which applies not only to the shared authority between pope and bishops but also to the structures of the national conferences of bishops where the chairman is the first among peers. It also applies to the diocese: the bishop must listen to his *presbyterium*. The Synod of Bishops assisting the pope and the senate assisting the bishops are strictly analogous. The principle must also find implementation in the life of the parish and in religious orders. Therefore, the insights that were deepened and stressed at the extraordinary Synod of Bishops in October 1969 will have their impact on all levels in the church.

It cannot be denied that the language of the chapter of the *Dogmatic Constitution on the Church* relative to the hierarchy is not the most felicitous. While the text does open the door to new structures embodying greater freedom and demythologizing the Constantinian style of authority, the language is to a certain extent still the same old terminology. The wording shows how difficult it is to turn decisively away from the past. But the direction is clear, as Pope Paul VI has emphasized several times: "Authority in the church is nothing else than a service of love and salvation."

Christian freedom is a fruit of the Gospel in Jesus Christ.

The bishops, and with them priests, will truly be servants of freedom if they make the proclamation of the Gospel and the witness to the Gospel their chief concern. Vatican II declares with great emphasis that for this mission they receive the power of the Holy Spirit and by fulfilling it they are servants of the People of God. "Now, that duty which the Lord committed to the shepherds of His people is a true service, and in sacred literature is significantly called 'diakonia' or 'ministry.'"[6] "Among the principal duties of bishops, the preaching of the Gospel occupies an eminent place."[7] "In exercising their duty of teaching they should announce the Gospel of Christ to men, a task which is eminent among the chief duties of bishops."[8]

The proclamation of the Gospel as the chief task of bishops and the glorification of God "in Spirit and truth" should have heartening results: the council mentions, in the first place, the freedom of the human person: "Hence let them teach with what seriousness the Church believes these realities should be regarded: the human person with his freedom and bodily life. . . ."[9]

Tensions between the Old and New Styles

Since we live in a time of transition, nobody should be surprised that not all bishops have as yet acquired a manner

[6] *Dogmatic Constitution on the Church*, Art. 24.
[7] *Ibid.*, Art. 25.
[8] *Decree on Bishop's Office in the Church*, Art. 12.
[9] *Ibid.*

of speaking and a conception of their ministry fully in accord with the perspectives set forth in the council. There are still classic examples of old-style Germanic or Irish prince-bishops around. Suspensions and excommunications are fulminated when differences could more easily be settled simply by modifying the style of authority. Archbishop Lucey's behavior, in his controversy with Father McKenzie, is a good example of the dichotomy between power and love which is at the roots of the present crisis of authority. The present tensions in the archdioceses of Washington and Florence might eventually have quite an impact on the learning process now going on in the church with regard to the proper understanding of church authority. The investigation of Monsignor Illich, handled so inexpertly by the old faction in the Holy Office, came as quite a shock to many. The fact that such instances of episcopal failure are today given the widest publicity may help us to rectify more quickly the discrepancy between the outlook of Vatican II and that older attitude toward authority which is neither evangelical nor modern; in fact, it reflects a style of thinking commonly found in nineteenth-century Europe as well as the Middle Ages. The fact that Paul VI twice visited Patriarch Athenagoras before inviting him to Rome is a hopeful sign that the church of the new age will realize that brotherhood and humility must be the chief characteristics of the exercise of ecclesiastical authority today.

Much will depend upon how the canon law is reformed. Will it, under the liberating power of the Gospel, express, protect and foster that style of authority that can be considered a genuine "incarnation" of the new age? The canonists of the old school have a hard time understanding the very nature of the above-mentioned changes. However, there are canonists who have enough background in theology and sociology to make progress in the right direction. The Canon Law Society of the United States is a symbol of realistic hope. The Synod of Bishops meeting in Rome in the fall of 1967 reaffirmed the spirit of Vatican II with regard to the forms and norms desirable in a new code of canon law.

Theology in the Service of True Freedom

With regard to structural changes, theologians were rather modest in their hopes at the time of Vatican II. Even so, some unfriendly words were said about them in St. Peter's. However, the council gave them a unique opportunity to fulfill their prophetic role in the church. As a result, there is real hope that the ossification of a theology that simply quoted the *Enchiridion* according to Denzinger will be overcome. There is now a greater and more general awareness of the history of salvation, of the pilgrim character of theology as well as of the whole church. The important function of the Magisterium will be seen more and more in a historical context. The ecumenical spirit and ecumenical dialogue, which will be found more and more in our theological seminaries and in theology as a whole, will be more generous in evaluating the complementarity of different theologies belonging to different cultures and epochs. The decree on *Priestly Formation* as well as the decree on *Ecumenism* are encouraging theologians to think along these lines: "Dogmatic theology should be so arranged that the biblical themes are presented first. Students should be shown that the Fathers of the Eastern and Western Churches contributed to the fruitful transmission and illumination of the individual truths of revelation and also the later history of dogma and its relation to the general history of the Church. . . . Let the students learn to search for solutions to human problems with the light of revelation, to apply eternal truths to changing conditions of human affairs, and to communicate such truths in a manner suited to contemporary man."[10]

The Dutch Catechism for adults can be considered an example of how seriously some parts of the church at least take this business of communications. But it is also typical, of course, that some men of the old school have shown nothing but contempt for this effort and did not even consider a revision of it worthwhile. A battle is still going on between those who want above all to be "safe" by repeating eternally the old formulas and those who want to communicate evangelical truths vitally in the language of contemporary man.

Vatican II has given theologians a magna charta that will have an impact not only on the freedom of creative theologians but on the spirit of Christian freedom in the church as a whole: "In order that such persons [theologians] may

---

[10] *Decree on Priestly Formation*, Art. 16.

fulfill their proper function, let it be recognized that all the faithful, clerical and lay, possess a lawful freedom of inquiry and of thought and the freedom to express their minds humbly and courageously about those matters in which they enjoy competence."[11]

This Article 62 is in the chapter on culture. It shows a vital awareness that the church cannot inspire and promote freedom, so necessary for all human culture and especially for modern culture, unless she first embodies in a convincing way this very spirit of freedom in her own life. Culture is understood as the development of freedom and of awareness in freedom. "Because it flows immediately from man's spiritual and intellectual nature, culture has constant need of just freedom if it is to develop. It needs the legitimate possibility of exercising its independence according to its own principles. Rightly, therefore, it demands respect and enjoys a certain inviolability, at least as long as the rights of the individual and of the community, whether particular or universal, are preserved within the context of the common good."[12]

Ethics of Responsible Freedom

The ethos underlying the whole *Constitution on the Church in the Modern World* is one of responsibility in freedom. Only mature Christians can give witness and fulfill their

[11] *Church in the Modern World*, Art. 62.
[12] *Ibid.*, Art. 59.

role in a pluralistic, dynamic society. Suffice it to quote here what is said about conscience: "Conscience is the most secret core and sanctuary of a man. There he is alone with God whose voice echoes in his depth. In a wonderful manner conscience reveals that law which is fulfilled by love of God and neighbor. In fidelity to conscience, Christians are joined with the rest of men in the search for truth and for genuine solutions to the numerous problems which arise in the life of individuals and from social relationships. . . ."[13] If conscience is king, Christians will give to those in authority a mature obedience, which is so much more than a mere dependence on authorities. It will always and above all be an expression of responsibility, of concern for the good of neighbor and of the whole community.

The Liberating Power of the Gospel

The *Declaration on Religious Liberty* represented a tremendous effort on the part of the council to liberate the church from the terrible consequences of the dual role of Emperor and Pontifex Maximus (highest religious authority) as found in Constantine and his successors, the old Germanic idea of absolute allegiance to princes who determined the religion of their subjects, and imperial bishops who similarly confounded the spiritual and the temporal in their claims to "absolute allegiance."

[13] *Ibid.,* Art. 16.

VIII

The Missionary Dimensions of Protest

Christian ethics is not an area coexisting beside, or outside, faith. Rather, it is the inner radiance of faith itself. It is the dynamism of the joy of faith, of the conviction of faith and of an attitude of faith that ceaselessly constrains one to witness for the faith in one God, Creator, Father and Redeemer of all men. Salvation comes from faith alone, not, however, from a faith that is merely the intellectual assent to propositions of faith. Faith means festive reception of the saving truth, a grateful affirmation of Christ who is the Way, the Truth and the Life of all men. Faith means giving oneself completely to the one Lord Jesus Christ, who desires to gather all the world into the Kingdom of the Father's love. Faith means being united with Christ who desired to carry the burden of all his brothers and sisters and who came to bring salvation to all. Ethics, understood in a Christian sense, is the dynamism and vital truthfulness of faith. Thus understood, Christian ethics is always a converting sermon directed to a Christendom which has all too little radiance, to a Christendom which has often lost itself in a thousand microscopic minutiae of the law or in trivial matters, and has treated the last will and testament of our Lord "that all might be one" as something altogether of secondary importance.

Two quite distinct lines of thought occurred to me under the title, "Une contestation missionnaire de la morale chrétienne" (the missionary challenge of Christian ethics and to Christian ethics). On the one hand, I believe that the morality which we have taught and in part practiced requires a mighty prophetic challenge if it is to become really missionary in nature. On the other hand, I recognize that the whole moral theology of the church has the task of awakening all Christians and ecclesiastical institutions to a deeper missionary concern.

The Missionary Challenge to a Static Ethics

Mission is the radiating power of faith, the message of salvation directed to everybody. The messenger of faith goes to men wherever they are to be found. He preaches faith before he preaches moral commandments. He does not try to reap the harvest before he has credibly sown the word of faith.

Our moralists should honestly ask themselves whether they have always given the primacy to faith. Have they not, by planting a thicket of all kinds of laws, almost all "under deadly sin," diminished the joy of faith and consequently the radiant power of Christian missions? Have they not sometimes preached an ethic of self-perfection in a Stoic or Aristotelian sense instead of an ethic of devotion, of faith and witness of faith? Undoubtedly, much could be said about that; one needs only to read the traditional textbooks on moral theology. I do not believe that the moralists, in the face of a world crying out for Christ, a world which has not been won by our mission, can defend themselves by saying: "Did we not also, in a few lines or paragraphs, indicate that Christians should support missions?" The question is rather: Was the whole structure of this "Christian ethic" missionary, winning, radiant? Did this ethic offer a great guiding ideal or a great leitmotif which could awaken Christendom to missionary zeal?

The morality proclaimed in our schools and sermons was to an excessive degree a static morality, a morality merely of restrictive and prohibitive commands. It failed to translate into life the dynamics of the directives of sacred scripture. To a large extent, it even distorted them into counsels with no binding force. Morality forced the Christian to become a self-provider. The one-sided emphasis on individual duties concealed both social goals and those goals resulting from salvation.

The morality of the Bible is a morality which abhors complacency and the mere ensuring of the status quo. The morality of the New Testament is a morality of perpetual conversion, both of the individual and of society. The morality of the Bible is a morality of the joy of faith. Its norm is comprised in the Beatitudes, in the joyful proclamation of the joyful message. Morality is through and through part of the joyful message itself. Is it not true that theologians have all too often transformed the joyful news into a "castrated dogmatic formula" and placed alongside it sterile moral imperatives, imperatives which seemed to have nothing in common with dogma understood as joyful news? As a consequence, has not morality lost its radiance and attractiveness?

In addition to these fundamental complaints which touch in particular that kind of moral theology and moral preaching which is now, with surprising rapidity, becoming extinct, there are many particular complaints which relate to contemporary efforts in moral theology. Has not church morality been too monopolistic? Naturally, Christian morality must constantly stress the unique place of Christ. Has it really done this well? It may never dare leave in doubt the mission of the Catholic Church to the whole world. But it is a different matter with systems of thought which have their origin in Greek philosophy, in Roman methods of ruling and in the old Germanic ideal of the absolute obedience of subjects.

The education in ethics which we gave to our missionaries was largely a mixture (seemingly unproblematical) of elements taken from the Gospel and from the Roman practice of law. It mirrored the culture of peoples living near the Mediterranean. Our ethics were far too European. The ease with which we declared that our own particular customs and conceptions were the eternal law of nature was not only a sign of our ignorance of other cultures and traditions but also a mirror of our European pride. We held ourselves to be "the cultured people" while we left to others only the right to learn from us and be instructed by us.

The moralists who so precisely distinguished between servile and nonservile work on Sundays, who labeled everything "mortal sin" or "venial sin," did not dare speak up when ecclesiastical authorities and organizations declared the Latin language and Latin culture to be *"sopracultura"* and ascribed to the church the task of civilizing the barbarians with the aid of Latin theology and the Latin liturgy. In a word, our morality did not apply to relations with other cultures the basic doctrine of humility and docility. Morality itself was too complacent.

I still have a lively memory of the horror and fright in Rome about twenty years ago when a learned Vietnamese frankly and openly said to one of the most charming of our canonist-moralists, "If you have nothing better to offer us than this mixture of unadjusted canon law and European formulations of natural law, please stay home; the ethic of Confucius seems to me to be closer to the Gospel." Despite the critical attitude I already held relative to the mingling of morals and canon law, I protested that challenge. The Vietnamese asked me in a friendly way whether I had read

the ethics of Confucius; when I said I had not, he brought
me *The Four Holy Books of Confucius* and begged me to
read it before judging his harsh verdict. When I read it, I
realized that we can actually learn much from it. The
Chinese system of four cardinal virtues—Confucianism
speaks of the "four most precious gifts which heaven confers
on the wise man"—is closer to evangelical ethics than the
Greek system, which has no place for either graciousness or
courtesy and focuses too much on one's own self-perfection.

In mystical-ascetical theology we have rightly set forth
docility vis-à-vis the grace of the Holy Spirit as a basic attitude. But in the *Institutiones theologiae moralis* there was
scarcely a word to be found to the effect that docility to the
Holy Spirit embraces readiness to learn wherever the Spirit
of God is at work. We know that readiness to hear is a basic
attitude of the man of faith. But our ethics has not made
clear that the proclamation of the Gospel and of the joy-
giving moral message to other people and to other social
classes and other cultures presupposes first of all readiness to
listen to these people and to appreciate their culture. We
remained unable to say this because we moralists were also
infected with this sense of superiority of our European or
national culture.

Another reproach no less grave is that the ethics presented
to seminarians in many manuals reflected the rearguard of
the culture and social class of an ecclesiastical group concerned above all with the maintenance of the status quo.
Clinging to the old was equated with virtue. Sins were
looked for and were severely rebuked in a one-sided way

critical of venturesomeness or of courageous attempts to tread new paths. This was associated not only with a lopsided stress on restrictive laws but also with an institutional and affinitive alliance with the ruling class, with the feudal nobility and later with the bourgeoisie. Consequently, ecclesiastical ethics was not missionarily alive to the decisive movements and endeavors of the west. Ecclesiastical ethics was largely oriented toward defending the clerical monopoly of culture and science against the laity, to defending clerical privileges by means of a holy alliance with the nobility, all in the name of Christ. This kind of shortsighted ethics reproved the thoughtless mention of the name of God on the part of the little people, but said practically nothing about the sin of those who frivolously appealed to authority, to the name of God and to the eternal law of God, when their real concern was narrowly only with their own privileges or petty interests.

This ethics proved insufficiently prophetic as a strident conservative group forced the supreme leaders of the church to make Latin rites and practically the whole Latin way of thinking the universal law—in practice, the universal obstacle—of missions. The kind of loyalty we find in the Bible should have obliged moral theologians, by pleas and entreaties and all they could helpfully do, to clarify constantly to the leaders of the church and to bring to public consciousness the concerns of the missionaries. The moralists should not have chosen the easy way of appealing one-sidedly to an obedience in which concern for the missionary apostolate of the church to all peoples found insufficient expression.

The moral theology of the last century sanctioned the individualistic concept of private property as entertained by the ruling class and by an individualistic European culture. Christian ethics, which above all should cultivate the discernment of spirits, was for a long time uncritical with regard to this individualistic concept of property and its many effects. The moralists were uncritical not only because they had grown up in this climate and for the most part came from the bourgeoisie, but also because they themselves knew little about the missionary apostolate of the church to all classes and all cultures. As a consequence, a terrible scandal occurred when the church in many countries lost the working class. Moreover, this individualistic concept of private property was utterly alien to most African and Asian cultures. How could such an individualistic, European ethic of private property make credible to more socially oriented cultures faith in the one Creator and Giver of all gifts and in the one Redeemer Jesus Christ?

One of the main reasons for the magnetic power of the church during the earliest Christian centuries was the sublimity and superiority of the Christian ethics of marriage and the family. There is no doubt that Christian moral theology made a contribution both to the emancipation of women and to respect for women as well as to a deepened understanding of the ethics of marriage and family. But have the moral theologians really made a serious attempt to distinguish in marriage ethics and marriage law the specifically Christian elements from those elements which were more or less a successful accommodation to European culture?

In many letters I have received and in numerous discussions, particularly in East Africa, I have come across a wholesome kind of protest. Missionary bishops, native, European and American missionaries have reproached moralists for their failure to pay sufficient attention to the question of evangelizing polygamous peoples and for providing ready-made answers before they had really studied the situation. God, they argued, took his time in educating Israel, beginning with Abraham, Isaac and Jacob, right through to David. He took time to educate our fathers in the faith in their understanding of absolute monogamy. The moralists, however, demanded that tribes in which a moderate form of polygamy is culturally and economically deeply rooted should embrace monogamy before the Gospel could be preached to them.

Fr. Hillman, an American missionary to the Masai of Tanzania, speaks for many missionaries and for many men and women who desire to be baptized, but without acting contrary to their conscience, which is differently formed from ours. The Masai who has remained faithful to his two wives, and who has taken care of the mother of his children to the best of his ability and successfully, cannot believe that in order to be baptized he must in the name of God break the contracts which he and two extended families have confirmed, and drive the mother of his children into destitution, which in many cases means forcing her into prostitution. Must he really, in order to honor God, renounce his honor with the members of his tribe? Not only are these conditions hard for him, but they make it extraordinarily difficult for him to believe the Gospel. Why should missionaries demand this, seeing that God himself who selected Abraham to be our father in faith employed a totally different method of education?[1] The urgent question for the moralists is not whether they can offer a ready-made solution. The real protest lies in the question whether they have ever really seriously thought about this and similar questions which are of such decisive importance in many missionary situations. Are they disturbed by the thought that their solutions for the ethics of the confessional are milder for the roaming polygynist who every year has sexual intercourse with several women besides his legitimate wife—and this in countries with a long Christian tradition—than for the respectable man of the polygynistic culture who wants to become a Christian?

The pressing question is of a more general nature. It is the question whether they have really examined the situation in the light of the "law of faith." Would not perhaps this law of faith suggest that we receive such men with their culture into the community of faith and then trust to the dynamism of faith? Along with many diverse hygienic, economic, social and cultural transformations faith would, as it did in Israel, exert its transforming power and lead to monogamy. The protest offers not theses but questions.

The Old Testament sanctioned leviratical marriage, an institution conditioned by the culture of the age (cf. Gen. 38). Onan was punished with death by God because he

---

[1] Cf. Eugene Hillman, C.S.Sp., "Polygyny Reconsidered" in *Concilium*, III, 1968, pp. 80–89.

sought to evade his levirate duty toward the widow of his brother. This duty was enjoined by the law even in cases where the brother-in-law of the widow was already married. Must the missionary obey the moralist and deny the sacraments to a Christian married man who with considerable sacrifices fulfills his levirate duty toward the widow of his brother, and to the widow who adheres to this order demanded by tribal custom in order that she may not be robbed of her children and lose her place in the tribe? He will do this even when conjugal intercourse is reduced to a radical minimum. Once more the primary question of those who contest this morality is: Have you moralists thought as earnestly about this question as about the imposition of the smallest rubric instructions?

The catalogue of complaints is by no means complete. This is merely a small sampling. Are the voices loud enough to induce the moral theologians at least to begin to devote themselves to the development of a missionary moral theology, of a more catholic, worldwide ethic?

Acceptance of Challenge and the Courage to Challenge

Is it right for us moral theologians of the present generation to bear all the responsibility for the past? We certainly deserve a good share of the wholesome protests that may help to awaken us from our slumbers. But to the extent that we are aroused, we must also feel compelled to utter a word of entreaty.

Why do not missionary societies and missionary bishops urge influential moral theologians, and especially promising young moral theologians, to visit missionary areas from time to time, to participate in instruction courses there, to join in discussions, to expose themselves to the questions and complaints? Reading scientific works and receiving letters which I take very seriously has not impressed me personally nearly as much as personal contacts with various missions.

It was from the mission field that Reformation churches received the first effective stimulus to an ecumenical revolution. Similarly, the Catholic bishops from Africa and Asia played a major role at the Second Vatican Council. Without them the council would have been unable to achieve a certain opening toward a more worldwide and truly catholic way of thought. Still, my question to the missionaries and Christians of these countries is whether they have sufficiently considered how far the Mediterranean character of our ethics and canon law has rendered their efforts and endeavors in part unfruitful. To the extent that they are already aware of these problems, have they done all they could to force the leading organisms of the church and, more importantly, moral theologians to study their problems with real seriousness?

The aim of all genuine protest in the church should be the strengthening of dialogue. We are witnessing a large number of protests of this kind. Often, however, such protests remain a mere complaint, a mere experience of frustration, an outburst of criticism which fails to reach the partner in the dialogue. The purpose of protest should be to draw attention to some important concern and to reach a fruitful dialogue in order to clear a path for the future.

If, however, we allow ourselves to get involved in noisy protests over all kinds of minor matters and devote little attention to Christ's great missionary mandate, it is clear that our protest effort itself needs to undergo a missionary conversion.

Moral theology faces many difficult questions relating to those for whom our ethical formulations have created real problems of faith. Moral theology must be rethought and reformulated with a view to ecumenical dialogue and not least in the light of the need to work out a total view of moral theology which can serve a truly missionary church and can render that church even more missionary-minded. Moral theologians must begin to treat many delicate questions arising from the missionary situation. In order to do so, however, they need an atmosphere of support, i.e., one of freedom and cooperation on the part of church authorities. That *parresia,* that frankness and courageous concern for burning questions which we find in the Bible, has been largely ignored by the church in past centuries. The fault was not that of moral theologians alone. For while moral theologians were permitted to make many grotesque "deviations to the right" that gravely damaged the reputation and missionary radiance of the church, all too often almost every attempt to move forward was dubbed *a priori* a dangerous "deviation to the left." But moral theologians should have both sufficient virtue and sufficient humor not only to absorb protests from the right and from the left, but also to receive *monita* from church authorities patiently, with humor and in a spirit of self-criticism. If we want the community of moral theologians to join the avant-garde of a missionary church, we must provide the right mixture of protests and official warnings with encouragement and the establishment of appropriate structures for dialogue on all levels within the church and among all mankind.

IX

The Hope in Protest

Not all problems relating to authority and protest can be solved by merely knowing what factors have precipitated the crisis. With respect to the present situation in the church, it is of the utmost importance to honor God, the highest Authority, with trust by hoping much from him, believing that he can always write straight on crooked lines.

I tend to agree with C. S. Lewis with regard to the unified strategy of the Supervisor of Devils who exhorts his demons to be true to their vocation of spreading pessimism. They are enjoined to use a mixture of pious talk aimed at preserving church structures while making the very Church of Christ a sacrament or instrument of pessimism.

We have to protest, in the name of God and on God's authority, against all manifestations of resentment and despair, against any exercise of authority that reveals cowardice or lack of trust in God, and against any kind of protest that is merely a cry of despair. Authority is powerless to act unless it can inspire trust and is not even recognized as authority unless it is received with trust. Protest has meaning only if it is inspired by greater hope.

Protest Inspired by Hope

I am on the side of Teilhard de Chardin, whose fundamental position is that the world belongs to those who can offer it greater hope. We can generally say that youth and youthful men and women involved in protests are those who still have that greater hope. Only a correct understanding of trust and hope enables us to distinguish an erratic uproar or an outcry of despair and destruction, i.e., pessimism, from the kind of protest that is inspired by hope. Protest is genuine only if it is adoration of that One and Unique Authority challenging all secondary authorities that dare "to take the place of God" instead of making a place for him.

Protest is a challenge for us to differentiate between God's authority and those mediating God's authority, whose role therefore is properly one of being "servants." Christ challenged all human authority by revealing the authority of his Father through his own service. He manifests the heavenly Kingdom, the One who governs and guides by his love, by submitting himself to be the mediator of this authority.

Therefore, God has exalted him and given him a name, an authority that is above all authorities.

Hope is the great theme of all masterly literary works of our time; they all express hope or despair. Take Camus; you may consider him a man without faith. He plays an influential role in explaining the chaos of meaninglessness, but if you look closely at his entire works and his real character, you can still detect a tremendous desire for meaningfulness, which is existence in love.

Accepting Authority

We cannot speak about authority without implying an acceptance of authority. I refrain from using the term "obedience" because it implies slavishness and a certain unreasonableness. However, what I mean is the genuine Christian virtue of obedience in faith, mature obedience. Protest is treated only insofar as we can distinguish genuine authority from the counterfeits of authority.

Authority exists only where people exercise an authority of love and salvation and where people have trust in this authority and believe in this authority. All great realities have to be understood in this dialectical form. This is especially true of trust. God gives credit to man by making him a sharer in his freedom, by making him a mediator, an instrument, a witness of his authority, but at the same time God protests if man does not respond in trust, i.e., in fidelity to what is entrusted to him. Christian trust and hope are a dialectical concept and only if we understand the concept in this way can we relate it to the dialogical responsorial concept of authority and genuine obedience.

Man becomes trusting and hopeful to the extent that he has experienced trust, goodness and kindness. Only then can he somehow hope for and desire the greater fulfillment of goodness and kindness. A child will grow up and come to the fullness of Christian optimism, hope, trust and faith to the extent that he is an accepted child, a beloved person. If from the very beginning the child is not wanted or is not accepted in trust, then throughout his life he will need a great deal of community attention to give him the trust and credit of which he seems to be unworthy but of which he wants to become worthy.

Look at the countenance of a child. If he is joyous and happy, you know that he has parents who trust the Creator and give credit to the child. Their authority is one of love, having its origin in love and trust. Then turn to the sad countenance of another child and you know that he has not experienced an authority originating from love. He has not known an authority that caused him to trust in life. The Christian concepts of authority and hope are closely linked together.

Authority and Redeeming Love

God manifests his renewing authority by his promises and his fidelity to mankind when he finds them in need of redemption. The authority of hope abides in God's covenant, in the restorative and compassionate action of the Lord of history.

Theology should be constantly aware of the fact that there is no such thing in holy scripture as a treatise on original sin as such. God's denunciation of man's sinfulness and prophetic protest against man's solidarity in evil are always a sign of hope. Even judgment reveals that God never abandons interest in his people. God never leaves man without hope. Mankind is subjected to painful solidarity in Adam and Eve only in view of the saving solidarity in Christ. The existential character of the prophetic denunciation of man's solidarity in sin is always a call to conversion. And this summons makes clear that man cannot rid himself of collective despair except by accepting completely the call to solidarity in Christ. We find judgment of mankind as being subjected to the collective punishment which belongs to a sinful people only in an existential context, in the sense that God purifies his people and summons everyone to form part of a holy people. The biblical kerygma is, in tone and vision, totally different from an oversystematized presentation of the truth of original sin as we find it in theology since St. Augustine and even more so in recent scholasticism. These treatises are really like "frozen protests" or "protests" without hope and dynamic appeal. On the contrary, in the protests of God's prophets there is always present the dynamism of hope. We find an appeal to trust in God's mercy. They visualize mankind, scattered through selfishness and chained together in sinfulness, as experiencing the merciful presence of the One who saves through judgment. God's judgments are for those who believe there is a beginning of salvation, a call to fidelity because of God's compassionate fidelity. All this has its final meaning in Christ, who is the saving Protest and the fulfillment of all promises, the prototype of that solidarity which is the way of hope.

In Jesus Christ there was no ambivalence. In him there was the presence of the "yes." In him all the promises of God came to final fulfillment. Therefore, in him God too received the "Amen" (II Cor. 1:19–21). It is the dialogical character of hope and of authority: "In him there is the law and the covenant," says St. Justin, but he means the new law which is the authority of love. God guides us by his love. In Christ God speaks and it was. He entrusted himself: "Thou hast fashioned me a body. . . . Behold, I come to do thy will" (Heb. 10:5–7). He manifests the authority of the Father in the final trust, the final manifestation of the acceptance of God's saving authority on the Cross. "Father, in thy hands I commend my spirit" (Luke 23:46). It is essential to note the word "Father" here. There was always the presence of the Covenant; there was always God's appeal to commend oneself to God but through Christ who is fullness. He commended himself as the Son, in full trust in the Father. This is hope and it is authority.

Hope is not man's own possession. When man relies upon himself, he finds the absolute beginning of pessimism. When man claims to be his own authority, there is emptiness, because he does not accept his true self, which is a call of God's originating love. Only through the gracious manifestation of God's own love, through grace, can man grasp God's authority, can he grasp hope.

The greatest realization of hope is in the Paschal Mystery, the extreme suffering, the sharing in the suffering of all mankind connoted by this mystery; there Christ expresses the authority of the Father and his trust in that redeeming authority. There he spoke the "Amen," that final acceptance of God's authority and final response to it in the name of all mankind.

We can say that there is a sacramental understanding both of authority and of hope. Genuine authority is said to be in action when love, loving care and fidelity become visible. It is a sacrament; it becomes visible, man can experience it. A sacrament is always a sacrament of faith. It truly comes about only when man wants to perceive that gift of saving authority to which he entrusts himself. A sacramental understanding does not mean the simultaneous "yes" and "no" of ambivalence, but a beginning "yes," a first manifestation which is a divine pledge of the final fulfillment.

Christ's authority comes on a donkey, the symbol of the humble people receiving everything with gratitude. He comes in the Paschal Mystery, in his humility, his solidarity, but he is the promise, the divine security that everything will come true. When he has himself surrendered to the Father, which includes both acceptance of the authority of the Father and total submission to him in love, he will submit everything to God, i.e., all who are united in him. In Christ and with him, those who accept the Father's authority and entrust themselves to the Father become sharers in God's own mercy, kindness, initiative, genuine freedom.

The church is a sacrament of hope but her sacramentality is subject to divine authority, subject to God. Christ warns, for instance in Luke (chapter 17, verse 32): "Remember Lot's wife." Where the church is backward-looking, where she yields to a security complex, where with a wrong slant toward authority she wants to keep what cannot be kept in the name of the Lord of history, she cannot be said to be the sacrament of hope. In such cases she needs protest, but protest from people who entrust themselves to the Lord of history. She needs protest from the ranks of the optimists.

The church in need of reform does not cease to be a sacrament of hope if she is truly aware of her need for reform, if she does not simply call herself the "reformed church" but "the church in need of reform." We constantly have to distinguish carefully between what God has offered us and what we have accepted. Thus the whole People of God have to distinguish between God's own authority, the real origin of love and fidelity, and the defective way in which we have responded to it. God remains faithful and continues to offer us remedies and punishments but by promising a Redeemer to help us.

Those parts of the church or of Christianity that appear to be mere establishments, precluding all protest against their being immobile establishments, have excluded themselves from the Lord of history, from the authority of freedom and the authority of hope. Therefore, we have to look on all ramparts of wrong authority such as inappropriate laws, frozen doctrinal formulas, ecclesiastical palaces, ecclesiastical diplomacy, cowardly prudence, cowardly groups—we have to distinguish all such things from the essence of the church on pilgrimage, the servant of God, subject to the One who inspires hope. As long as the church, the very heart of the church, confesses daily: "Forgive us the wrongs we have done as we forgive those who have wronged us," in spite of her sins she will remain a sacrament of hope, a sacrament of trust, and we dishonor her if we see only signs that frighten us.

Christian hope recognizes the defects and obstacles, but it takes the courage of hope to look at these defects and not be disheartened by them. Christian hope renders thanks to God who is always greater than our achievements, who has always offered us more than we have accepted and who will continue to offer himself to us. This should be the meaning of the church's sacramental authority. It does not operate magically. There is visibility, the splendor of God's dynamic presence whenever the priestly People of God entrust themselves to God and then make something visible—not their own authority—but God's authority. Thus they become those who have entrusted themselves, those who exercise their own humble authority, those who make visible God's greater authority.

Authority in Service

All authority is a service on behalf of the community. There is so much tension and so much need of protest today because officeholders and bearers of authority think only in terms of their own individual power or those who should be submissive to authority see it only with a view to their own individual wishes. The genuine approach to authority is solidarity in Christ, from which all other forms of solidarity flow. This is very evident in Christian hope.

Whenever man engages in a monologue, as in that marvelous literary passage in Genesis where man wants to be like God and where woman seeks domination over man, there we encounter the pessimism of the individualist. We have the links of solidarity that chain the egotists together in despair. We have hell.

The authority of God, on the other hand, is a rallying call or summons. The church has authority only to the extent that she gathers us all in Christian solidarity where our hope is based on the one reality that there is One who bears our burdens, who identifies himself with all of us who are sinners. Christ entrusts himself to the Father while fulfilling his role, his mission, namely, that of opening his arms to all of mankind. He did not come to please himself; he came to be the ransom for all, and this is the basis of reconciliation; this is the foundation of hope.

Hope does not shine forth in those forms of Christianity where everyone is just concerned with finding his own pious corner to save his own bodiless soul, where salvation is just a matter of finding the mercy of God for oneself. This is the real origin of alienation. Authority is the one God and Creator, the one Lord Jesus Christ who has come to bear the burdens of all, and the Holy Spirit who has anointed Christ for the task of being the servant of all and thus the servant of God. So Christian hope means striving for the perfect Kingdom, that heavenly Jerusalem, the communion of the saints, the sharing in God's love and thus the sharing in brotherhood.

All despair, all pessimism come from egotism and isolation. It is an act of despair, of pessimism for a Christian to say: "Let us leave behind us all of the institutionalized church." The latter, true, because of human weakness, may call for some form of protest, but what of all the efforts of the institution to gather our services for God, to gather us in worship, to gather us for the service of mankind?

It was one of the achievements of *The Pastoral Constitution of the Church in the Modern World* of Vatican II, which deals with the presence of the church in the world, to make clear that Christian hope, which is what we hope for, is perfect solidarity in Christ; this does not allow us to dissociate ourselves from any man, from any hope and joy, from any anguish or suffering of mankind. We will have courage to begin all over again, to help people, to relieve suffering by increasing brotherhood, only if our hope is genuine, only if we believe in oneness in God and in Christ.

Authority, Faith and Hope

We accept God's authority in faith. Faith is a joyous, humble and grateful acceptance of God's saving authority and presence and the entrusting of ourselves to his saving presence and his saving truth. We cannot define or describe faith apart from trust. We cannot describe God's authority apart from faith and trust, for it is not an authority that imposes itself by crushing man or eliminating him but one that awakens man and makes him a listener and a sharer in love.

Christian hope is not something added to faith any more than it is something added to authority. There is genuine authority only where there is a saving authority, a manifestation of love and salvation combined. Thus faith is, by its very essence, openness for all that God does in the present and what he promises in the future. It is a worshipping assent to all the saving deeds of God in the past, in the present and in the future. This is the description of faith found in St. Paul (Heb. 1:11). By its very essence, faith is a total entrusting of oneself, an openness to God's dynamic presence that constantly opens new horizons to us and that constantly surprises us; but the man who is faithful will become even more filled with hope by all the surprises that God actually brings him.

Abraham can truly be called our father in faith. He left behind him his family and his home. He left behind him a safe existence, as did Moses. He goes on pilgrimage entrusting himself to the Lord, a venturesome presence and truly an open future. In the same way the church will enjoy genuine authority if the life of each of the faithful and the life of the church as a whole are not dominated by that security complex which is content with formalism, with satisfaction with what grandfather did and what grandfather told us to do.

Christian hope is a dynamic thing; it is openness, pilgrimage, an adventure. Hope accounts for the many protests today against an immobile authority, an authority that claims to be the origin of life while remaining really sterile and immobile. That is why the protestors, to the extent that they are loving members of the People of God, have a role to play in authority by helping those in authority, that is, officeholders, to become more effectively, more visibly a genuine authority by accepting the challenge.

Faith is filled with hope and hope is filled with love. God reveals himself in creation and in Revelation; what he reveals is the splendor of his love. He is the authority of the church by means of the mission of the Holy Spirit. He sent the anointed One, Christ, to make manifest the fullness of his love. God thus makes Christ's friends able, through the power of the Holy Spirit, to grasp the presence of love and thus to become, in their turn, an instrument of peace and of love.

The saving love of God precedes our hope, and here the Christian definition of hope as love is very different from that of Aristotle and the Stoics, who stressed man's own *eros,* longing or desire for self-fulfillment. God is described as perfection and, therefore, the one who cannot love.

In the Christian message, God is described as the One who has compassion, the One who manifests himself as the origin of all love and life. Whenever he manifests himself, he brings to life genuine love, a genuine desire—not just for self-fulfillment—for becoming one with the origin of love. Thus the saving love of God precedes man's hope and man's trust.

We can say then that the origin of pessimism lies in self-trust, in self-complacency. All security complexes are the result of excessive trust in oneself. They are a refusal to accept the genuine risk of hope by entrusting oneself to God. The great risk is that the "old man" has to die, but he must trust that a new reality will come to life.

We do not generally tend to deny the truth of dogmatic definitions, statements of church doctrine, or the validity of church institutions, but all these things have to be accepted in openness, as evidences of our being on pilgrimage, as a means of entrusting ourselves to an ever greater hope, to an ever greater truth, to an ever greater God. God's love is truth, a saving truth that transcends infinitely all our formulations, all our approaches. Therefore, genuine understanding of Christian dogma, of Christian proclamation of the saving truth is to be seen in the very dynamism of love, in view of that love that shines forth now and that God wants to reveal finally.

It behooves us, then, to recognize for what it is the kind of faith that clings to dead formulas, the faith that is born dead or that has died, and the hope that is dead because of its selfishness. We must distinguish this kind of faith from a beginning of faith, a beginning of hope. Even if it is not filled in love, such faith knows about the origin of its being, namely, God's own love. Such faith is a constant openness to God's dynamic presence that leads us to a true faith, a true hope, a true opening to God's love and a genuine response. So the basis, the foundation of Christian faith and of Christian hope is the historical fact that God has called us into being and for no other reason than to have us as sharers in his own love, sharers in his own life, his own freedom, to the glory of his triune love, his love which is communally oriented, a rallying call, a summons.

The Authority of the Covenant

God has manifested his saving authority in the new covenant, which is not based on man's own achievement; it remains, it abides in spite of man's sins. Thus Christian hope is an awareness of our weakness but in the greater awareness of God's saving presence. The stability, the fidelity of hope is on the part of God; he is the authority, and thus hope is forward-looking to a fulfillment.

Christian hope also expresses itself in the way we understand Christian morality. Much could be said, but let us mention only one aspect here with respect to Christian tradition as we find it in the Bible. Some commandments are mainly prohibitive, that is, tell us not to do things which are opposed to love. Should these injunctions be the prime concern of a man of hope, a man who believes that his being draws its origin from God's infinite love and is directed by his authority toward a fullness of sharing? A truly Christian morality will not place the primary emphasis on prohibitive injunctions that would immobilize or frustrate man. The prime emphasis should be on commandments that manifest the final goal, as stated in the Sermon on the Mount: be all goodness as your heavenly Father is all goodness. The great commands of the sevenfold "But I say to you . . ." make us a pilgrim church, bring into our life a holy disquiet that never allows us to bask in a security complex. That command directs us to give trust to our brethren in view of the richness and depth of God's own love. We must not diminish our brethren by telling them merely what they are not allowed to do.

There must be this balance of trust, of hope expressing itself in the commandment goal "Thy will be done on earth as it is in heaven," even now in love. On the other hand, there must be an awareness, the courage of hope that allows us to see our imperfections, our sins, but in such a way that the horrifying aspects of our sins do not become stronger than the faith in God's power and love. This is the great danger of the pessimist, to become fixed about his weakness. He does not look on his own sinfulness with trust in God and in the presence of God. Therefore, he is still terrified because he remains self-centered. Christian morality should inspire trust and give credit to the other. It believes in the power of love, yet it humbly accepts the constant imperfections of man.

Christian existence is characterized by eschatological tension. God has already uttered his love; he has sent his *logos,* the wisdom of his love; we are all kept alive by his promises. We are already sons and daughters of God but with trust that by God's power and mercy this will become fully evident, the full reality that we are what we are called to be.

Therefore, of the Christian virtues, preeminence should be given to the eschatological virtues, and the greatest among these is hope. Hope is that faith which accepts the word of God as a message of salvation, a creative presence in the unique design, the great design wherein Christ is the point Omega and where his first coming in the flesh and his resurrection are an assurance of the final fulfillment. Therefore, Christian acceptance of authority is always open; God is still operating as Christ says: "My Father has never ceased his work, and I am working too" (John 5:17), and he will be that constant presence. He will remain with us even to the end of the world.

This is what we are called for and this is the humility and the courage of all mediating authority; this is constant openness. The church as a whole and the church in its prophetic men and women, the church as the People of God, gathered in solidarity by Christ, manifests to the world God's authority by their vigilance and by their openness to the present moment. By clinging to things of the past, men do not accept the present authority of God; it is a kind of alienation where we are always returning to formulations, to things that were true of the past, instead of looking to the present moment, learning from everything God has done in the history of salvation.

The eschatological virtue of hope is accompanied by a whole choir of other attitudes: vigilance, namely, alertness to the present coming of the Lord and allowing the Lord, since he is the Lord, to come in disguise, and by violent protest when we have not organized ourselves by means of nonviolent protest against all wrong forms of authority and all wrong kinds of establishment. The Lord may present himself in the form of discriminated-against brethren, in the form of people suffering from war or being exploited by the establishment.

Risk-taking Authority

Christian authority, Christian understanding of authority in the perspective of hope involves risk. A kind of despair is implied when a Christian ethicist or preacher excludes Christian courage and risk from his morality. Of course, it must be the genuine risk of love, the great venture of the Paschal Mystery. One who gives up his selfish self finds it, while one who clings to his selfish self wastes his true self. So much immaturity, so much wrong exercise of authority, comes from the very fact that we do not have enough trust, enough hope—hope in God and trust in man. We do not give credit to man.

In past centuries, at least in Catholic tradition and to some extent in others, insufficient place was accorded the virtue of *epikeia*. Aristotle, in explaining *epikeia,* says that one honors those in authority and the authority of law by looking first to the meaning, never clinging to a mechanical application of law. One dishonors authority by thinking there must be mechanism, a computerized fulfillment. One dishonors church authority particularly by insisting on this kind of mechanical obedience.

In the *Summa Theologica* (IIa IIae, Q. 120), Thomas Aquinas says: "It is vicious to cling to a literal obedience while the situation demands a more spiritual fulfillment." It is a vicious attitude toward church authority to be merely submissively or passively obedient. We honor church authority and indeed any genuine authority only by courageous obedience, obedience that looks for meaning, one that looks to everything in the great perspective of God's saving love, God's loving intention to save man, his authority, freedom, capacity to reciprocate love. Therefore, Christian hope as well as Christian authority and obedience must exclude a legalistic application of laws and authority. This calls for discernment.

If there is so much distrust, so much pessimism on the part of officeholders and other men, it is because we do not believe in the authority of the Holy Spirit. The great gift of the Holy Spirit is that of discernment, being able to recognize the One who has manifested to us the true countenance of love, Christ, the anointed One, the Lord.

The Heart of Authority Is Love

Christian hope is all-embracing—both those who protest and those who accept protest; it is always ready to strive for greater maturity, for a better discernment of what genuine love is, what a genuine exercise of authority and genuine obedience are. This includes, obviously, a constant readiness for conversion.

When the church, for the first time, became an established church under Constantine the Great and his successors, we had a great loving protest on the part of the monks. They had only one vow then, the constant readiness to change, to be converted, to accept the renewing action of the Holy Spirit. This is the essence of spirituality and it is one of the great eschatological virtues. Only thus can the church liberate herself from the appearance of being a dead establishment; and only those who, in their own lives, accept the great rule of the Sermon on the Mount, the whole teaching of Christ, the presence of the Holy Spirit, namely, a constant readiness to change—only such persons can preserve genuine authority and authentically manifest hope and trust.

Another of the great eschatological virtues is the spirit of humility or poverty as found in the first Beatitude. It is in the power of the Holy Spirit to make man realize that everything is God's gift. We must realize that God wants to give us ever-greater gifts. Since we recognize that we receive everything from God and the one Father in the one Redeemer, the spirit of poverty is always a spirit of service. The evangelical spirit of poverty must characterize the church in her reaching out to the world. The church then as a servant church, a church trusting in the Holy Spirit, will be an optimistic church. She will accept tensions, turmoil, disquiet, the pangs of childbirth, growing pains, because at the very heart of our hope, at the very heart of authority and of the One who is Lord, is the Paschal Mystery—the mystery of suffering, suffering accepted in trust and in solidarity with Christ, that redeems through love.

Postscript: Protest at the Synod

The meaning and importance of great events is sometimes brought home to us by certain incidents that take place, so to speak, on the sidelines. There was such a sideline issue, in my opinion, during the extraordinary Synod of Bishops in Rome in October, 1969—the press campaign against Cardinal Leo Joseph Suenens, the Belgian primate.

Doubtless the cardinal's famous interview granted to the editor of the French publication, *Informations Catholiques Internationales,* published last spring and almost immediately translated into at least eight languages, made quite an impact on world opinion. It certainly had a decisive influence on the Synod and its outcome, and many of Suenens' proposals and ideas were enthusiastically endorsed by bishops at the Synod. On the other hand, he was the target of severe criticism by a number of prelates. Many bishops regarded the cardinal's public airing of the critical situation in which the church now finds herself (particularly his blunt criticisms of the Roman Curia as responsible for much of the crisis) as unheard of and intolerable.

It is also known that certain circles in the Curia—we must be careful not to generalize—took a very dim view of the cardinal's interview. The echoes of Cardinal Ottaviani's famous remark during the council, "He who criticizes the Curia criticizes the Pope," have still not died away completely. Yet it is interesting that this point of view does not prevent certain conservative prelates, when it suits them, from indulging in spirited public attacks on the pope. One recent example of this was the highly critical and outspoken letter sent to the pope by the aged Curial Cardinals Ottaviani and Bacci, protesting against the changes in the mass scheduled to go into effect late in 1969. This will certainly not be the last protest from the conservative side.

As a result of his interview, Cardinal Suenens was not only the recipient of a batch of protest letters from fellow cardinals but the object of a well-organized press campaign. In one case at least, it is known that he was subjected to strong pressure by one high church official. The astonishing campaign launched against him during the Synod, especially by the rightist Italian press, bordered on the fantastic and hysterical. They even went so far, for example, as to invent the story of a sharp clash during the Synod between Cardinal Suenens and the Curial Cardinal, Dino Staffa, in a French-language workshop chaired by Suenens. Some journalists claimed that a knockdown controversy occurred, which was not the case at all. This must be acknowledged in fairness to Cardinal Staffa, who, according to one eyewitness, was completely positive and helpful throughout the discussions.

This whole storm of indignation raised by the liberal and neofascist press is an interesting example of a grotesque kind of "alienation of religion." Those responsible have provided us with a good example of a Marxist theory: the alienation of religion in practice. It is easy to reply to such attacks, for it is obvious that these rightist papers are not interested in religion at all. For them the important thing is their alliance with conservative forces in the church, which they maintain only to the extent that they believe the church can protect their social privileges. This explains their lamentation that Cardinal Suenens is trying to destroy the monarchical constitution of the church and their claim that this is the reason for his attack on the curial establishment. These rightist papers make no bones about revealing what they consider the real issues: they are above all *for* the Holy See's diplomatic service; *for* the monopoly of this service and of the secretariat of state by conservative prelates; *for* the monopoly of all career posts in the church by Italian prelates, with the papal "throne" itself as the highest rung on the ladder. We are reminded of Mussolini's statement in the 1930s that the Catholic Church would be nothing but an oriental sect were it not for the splendor of the Roman Empire, and his frank belief that it was worthwhile keeping up good relations with the church only to the extent that it contributed something of the splendor of the Roman Empire to Italy.

The most outrageous attack on Cardinal Suenens was concocted by the pornographic extreme-rightwing weekly, *Il Borghese,* which Cardinal Ottaviani favored with an exclusive interview over a year ago and which is continually "leaking" tidbits of gossip about high officials in the Vatican. Their attack on Cardinal Suenens, entitled "Who is Suenens?," not only was full of the usual insulting insinuations but also recounted absurd fictions as if they were common knowledge. A former fascist priest once said to me in all seriousness: "If there were nothing to it, *Il Borghese* would not publish it." The *pièce de résistance* of the article was to the effect that Cardinal Suenens had allegedly been unhappily married before entering the seminary and had put his wife in a convent. This "fact" is supposed to explain why the cardinal's views on sex and marriage are so avant-garde. They also alleged that he recently resumed contact with his wife, who is now an abbess somewhere. There are two pages full of this sort of trash. Of course, it is all pure invention. Cardinal Suenens entered the seminary at the age of sixteen.

It is amazing that *L'Osservatore Romano,* usually so concerned to defend the honor of "Princes of the Church," has so far made no comment on this shameful attack and on the besmirching of the cardinal's reputation. The reason certainly cannot be that those in the secretariat of state who direct the editorial policy of *L'Osservatore Romano* have not yet heard of the matter. It is known that the very day the article was published by *Il Borghese,* they had copies of it. We must ask ourselves: What are people to think about officials like this who on the one hand are behind a press campaign against Cardinal Suenens but at the same time certainly do not want to see it go so far as the article in *Il Borghese?* Their tactics prompt us to ask: What kind of a game are they playing?

Fortunately, it seems to me that sad experiences such as this can have a positive effect on the life of the church. God often writes straight on crooked lines. It has become all too clear how certain types of ecclesiastical careerism and diplomacy are intimately tied up with worldly desires and claims.

It will not do to investigate certain structures as mere abstractions; we must look upon them historically and in relationship to their concrete manifestations and ramifications. An appeal to the passions, such as in the case of the article in *Il Borghese,* can serve as a healthy shock.

When Pope Paul VI finally realizes the seriousness of what has happened and learns all the details—as I am sure he will—the completely hysterical and partisan nature of this press campaign against Cardinal Suenens can be utilized by him as a perfectly valid excuse to press ahead with much-needed reforms regarding offices, titles, promotions, methods of electing the pope, the accrediting of papal representatives to governments and episcopal conferences, and many other matters. Then the great efforts of Cardinal Suenens—directed toward restoring the spiritual credibility of the church, avoiding even the semblance of an alliance between papal diplomats and those circles that have a completely different outlook from that proposed by the encyclical, *Populorum Progressio,* and increasing the prestige of the Holy See by reorganizing the electoral college—will be more clearly and urgently seen for what they are.

Another aspect of the Synod that particularly struck me was the obvious connection between those who spoke against a clearly collegial exercise of the pastoral office and their sociological backgrounds and outlooks. The press has pointed out that the thrust of the proposals made by the Latin workshop, presided over by Cardinal Pericle Felici, was markedly different from that of the other language workshops. Doubtless this can largely be attributed to the special viewpoints and interests of certain curial circles, if not exclusively, for the Synod discussions showed that different currents of thought are represented even in the Curia. I am not referring to the kind of sociological and psychological outlook that a career in the Curia may be supposed to confer on certain individuals, but to the intimate relationship between *social* structures and ideas about *ecclesiastical* structures.

Archbishop Morcillo Gonzáles of Madrid is a good example of what I mean. His statement in an interview with the German church publication *Publik* to the effect that church teaching about collegiality forbids any collegial form of government for the church is in complete harmony with his known political ideals. He could hardly be expected to change his ideas about the way authority should be exercised in the church as long as he continues to regard the Caudillo's regime as the political ideal.

The way in which certain African bishops reacted to the interview of Cardinal Suenens and spoke out strongly on behalf of an even stronger exercise of papal authority at the Synod reveals the tribal origin of their thinking, even in some of the words they used: the uncontested authority of the tribal chief is vital for the well-being and unity of the tribe. In some of the newly formed African states, everything is going to pieces because they have not been able to achieve a strong central government. They therefore resist the tendency toward decentralization. Many other African bishops, on the other hand, are unusually sensitive to the possibilities of new democratic forms of government and the desire of certain elite groups for maturity and a greater scope for responsibility at all levels.

Cardinal Wyszynski's views, which stress the monarchical nature of the papal primacy and the role of the president of an episcopal conference, must be seen as historically conditioned. We have only to recall the period of the Roman persecutions—for example, the case of St. Cyprian, in third-century Africa. The authority of the bishop is quite naturally emphasized at such times, for obvious reasons. In times of persecution, when the church is fighting for its life, everybody appreciates the need for strong leadership. In the very dangerous Stalinist era, Cardinal Wyszynski embodied the authority and solidarity of a church that could not afford to allow its strength to be frittered away in idle discussions. Yet, when outside pressures let up, the tendency remains to cling to the same pattern of authoritarianism, even though this may hinder the widespread need for a newer outlook.

This reference to the connection between historical and sociological situations on the one hand, and the style of church authority on the other, may help us to understand better the present transformation of ideas about authority now going on in the church. Statements made by bishops in favor of improving the organization of the Synod do not necessarily mean that the old style is automatically being abandoned. The church meanwhile must become incarnate in the world *as it is*. It must try to work out methods and forms that will best make for collaboration between the successor of Peter and the College of Bishops in the great mission entrusted by Christ to his church.

Index

CARMELITE MONASTERY
Beckley Hill
Barre, Vt., 05641

DATE BORROWED

JUN 21 1970